MW00812682

Beyond Ophir

CONFESSIONS

of an

IDITAROD MUSHER, AN ALASKA ODYSSEY

JIM LANIER

Foreword by Joe Runyan

PO BOX 221974 ANCHORAGE, ALASKA 99522-1974
BOOKS@PUBLICATIONCONSULTANTS.COM—WWW.PUBLICATIONCONSULTANTS.COM

ISBN 978-1-59433-354-5
eBook ISBN 978-1-59433-355-2
Library of Congress Catalog Card Number: 2013-931663

Copyright 2013 Jim Lanier
—First Edition—

All rights reserved, including the right of
reproduction in any form, or by any mechanical
or electronic means including photocopying or
recording, or by any information storage or
retrieval system, in whole or in part in any
form, and in any case not without the
written permission of the author and publisher.

Cover Photo Courtesy of Al Grillo, grillophoto@gmail.com

Printed in Korea

Dedication

To Ron Gould

Foreword by Joe Runyan

Beyond Ophir: Confessions of an Iditarod Musher, Jim Lanier's self-effacing account of four decades of arctic adventure with sled dogs on the 1,000 mile Iditarod trail, conveniently occupied my reading evenings during the fall of 2012. Fortunately, not only was I asked to read the original manuscript, I was also asked to write the foreword for his book.

Why do I say fortunate? Well, I now have the opportunity to provide important information woefully absent in Jim's literary rendition which will allow the reader a clear understanding of one of Iditarod's iconic characters.

As Jim's former Iditarod and mushing colleague, and now a blogger who vicariously follows the Iditarod for race devotees, I was particularly interested in the subtle machinations of a dry witted mind, which I have appreciated for several decades. Of course, I understood that Jim Lanier was a doctor in Anchorage, but, honestly, I have only known him in an Iditarod setting encumbered in arctic clothes and by his all white team of Alaskan Huskies. Occasionally, I have caught him in a pedestrian way dressed in street clothes at a musher meeting or banquet, often with his wife Anna, whom I also know from the Iditarod trail. Over a period of time—I don't know exactly how it happened—I began to look forward to a chance encounter with Jim Lanier. This required some mental exercise to provide a topical subject because it was absolutely essential, from my point of view, to provoke or stimulate a pithy response in his low resonant baritone voice.

He does this in an even spoken professorial way, which initially masks the true identity of a guy with a monstrous sense of humor. For example, I saw Jim on the first floor of the Millennium Hotel on Thursday morning, just before the race start on the first Saturday of March 2012. I had not seen him since last year's race, but I realized that this first encounter was very important, and likely Jim will set me up with some easy fodder for my Iditarod blog if I can get him rolling.

Really, it's possible to say something stupid. I lead "Well, Jim, are you actually going to run an all-white team this year?" He answers very seriously, informs me that he was short on white dogs and actually will have some color coated huskies in the team, but within three sentences we are launched on a hilarious excursion into the existential reasons a guy 71 years old would be running his 15th Iditarod.

Having established the necessary repartee with Jim in Anchorage, and then standing for the magnificent a cappella of "The Star Spangled Banner" and "Alaska's Flag" (the Alaska State Song) by Jim, his wife Anna, and son Jimmy at the Thursday night Iditarod Banquet (Alaska's largest social event), I prepare myself for the trail and my job of journalizing the front running pack of the Iditarod.

In my 2012 narrative at Iditarod.com, I follow the lead pack of the Iditarod over the first third of the race from Willow, up the southern shoulder of the Alaska Range, down the north side of the great range through the intimidating Dalzell Gorge, and across the grand flats of the Nikolai Burn and the interminably immense Yukon River drainage.

For strategic reasons, race leaders Aliy Zirkle, the Older and the Younger Seavey, Burmeister, Baker, King, et al decide to stop about 100 miles short of the half-way point, the remote checkpoint of Cripple, for a mandatory 24 hour rest. Though the first musher to Cripple checkpoint will win $3,000 dollars in gold nuggets, the front runners decide to pull up in Takotna. Several considerations form their decision, but the biggest concern is the condition of the trail "Beyond Ophir" to Cripple checkpoint which is said to be windblown, soft, and slow pulling. The race leaders decide to stop in Takotna, rest their dogs, and hope that the trail will harden in the next 24 hours.

Behind Zirkle et al arrived musher after musher, all of whom decided to stop in Takotna. This drives me nuts because a situation has been offered to the middle of the pack to "seize the day" and vault passed the front of the race and Win The Gold. I kept asking anyone that would listen, "Where is the man or woman willing to take a gamble and go for the gold?" If you know you can't win the Iditarod, why not take a chance and forge on to Cripple?

Well, there are a couple of good reasons, one of which is that the first musher to Cripple will cross a truly primitive, stark, and uninhabited 77 miles of trail alone. If the trail, as reported, is a sugar bowl of loose snow, the mushing could be interminable. Yet, I just could not believe somebody would not step up to the plate and take the challenge.

At the Takotna checkpoint I continued to watch team after team pulling in to camp and refuse to challenge the front of the pack and move further down the trail. I circulated around the checkpoint kitchen looking for stories amongst dining mushers.

Finally, at 2:59 PM (March 7), almost 14 hours after the arrival of Aliy Zirkle, a cry went out that a musher was approaching the checkpoint. I stepped outside, immediately donning my sun glasses in the afternoon sun, looked through the glare, and noted the arrival of a nearly all white team of huskies. Jim Lanier.

I yelled out "A hero emerges!" While Jim signed the checker's sign in sheet, I asked, "Tell me you are going to get the half-way gold at Cripple." Jim looked at me contemplatively. At the same time I realized he was dead tired, pounded by the trail, and exhausted.

Yet, in the ensuing three seconds, a new raison d'etre was formed. With considerable conviction, he said, evenly, "I am not stopping. I am going to Cripple." For a moment I was astounded because Jim, often the oldest guy on the trail, had reason to stop.

I looked around the checkpoint crowd and dramatically stated, "That's our man, somebody has finally accepted the challenge and will forge alone to the halfway gold."

Jim repeated to the checker, "I am not stopping, I am going to Cripple." After only 8 minutes in Takotna, grabbing a sack lunch from the kitchen, he then pulled the hook anchoring his team, and the nearly all white team of huskies (A couple of them are various husky colors.) started the long climb on the old mining road bed to Ophir and then on to Cripple. I took a few photos for my next blog.

I started to think about Jim's chances of actually beating the front runners to Cripple. To be honest, it would be close since Jim would certainly stop for a rest in Ophir, a third of the way to the gold in Cripple. Realistically, "Beyond Ophir" he would probably find the trail soft and need to take another break mid-way on the expansive tundra to Cripple. Remember, the distance from Ophir to Cripple is huge—estimated by trail breakers at 77 miles.

Through the following night I blogged about Jim's chances to eclipse the front runners. One other musher, Trent Herbst, a middle of the pack racer, was also on the trail and seemed intent on the gold as well. Trent had pocketed the gold in 2011 by beating Kelly Griffin to Iditarod (halfway point on the southern route). He was like a hawk that flies over the same chicken coup for another chance at a meal. He could, I thought, catch Jim Lanier and put the gold in his personal exchequer, also accompanied by a quality photo with a long frosted beard.

I was really pulling for Jim and would check in with officials at the checkpoint and watch little green GPS dots identifying mushers march across the computer map of Alaska. By 10:44 AM the following morning, I was facing reality and wrote:

"YET, we have another difficulty. I think Mitch (Seavey, an Iditarod champ) and company, steam rolling off a magnificent 24 hour rest, with the best sled dogs in the world, following on relatively soft trail requiring lots of dog power, are going to eat Trent and Jim for breakfast. Bet on it if you want, but I think Jim and Trent are out of the money."

While Jim and team labored step by step in the most elemental and physical way, I flew ahead in an airplane to the remote checkpoint of Cripple, a collection of wall tents established every two years for the Iditarod. Here we waited for the first musher.

At 1:55 PM, March 8, Jim Lanier and team appeared on a long slough within view of a crowd of officials, pilots, and trail volunteers and trotted elegantly and first into Cripple. Eighteen minutes later, Mitch Seavey and his bullet train of huskies arrived second. By perseverance and raw will power, Jim had stymied the lead pack and pocketed the gold.

Congratulating him on his accomplishment, kidding him a little about stealing candy from babies, agreeing that his wife Anna was probably designing her gold nugget jewelry, he replied in a most serious tone, "I hope Jimmy (his fourteen year old son) is proud of me."

Knowing that part of my friend Jim Lanier, the reader may now explore a truly great read of life on the Iditarod trail.

Joe Runyan
1989 Iditarod Champ
Cliff, New Mexico

INTRODUCTION

For many years my wife, Anna, has encouraged me to take the time to chronicle my Iditarod and other related adventures, primarily for my children, and my children's children. So in April 2010, while convalescing from right hand surgery, I put pen in hand, my writing left hand, and began. It led to a process as enjoyable as the adventures themselves.

The final product, if such is ever final, may both inform and entertain. Well, at least entertain. The inform part rests somewhat contingent upon the degree to which I can adhere to historical veracity. After all, it's been decades since 1979, the book's backbone. Any lack of resemblance to the facts—people, places, events—besides unintentional, is of necessity under-standable, hopefully forgivable.

If at times the narration plods on and on, that may prove acceptable, imparting a realistic feel for the Iditarod, which can plod on and on itself. The plodding concludes in forty-nine mercifully short chapters, remarkably coincident with noteworthy numbers from the past. In 1959 Alaska became the forty-ninth state of the Union. Inspired by statehood, the Iditarod early on adopted 1049 miles as the official, if inaccurate, length of the race. Also, $1049 was for many years the race's entry fee, and $1049 is the amount returned from the entry to each entrant for making it to Nome.

Prolog

Now a checkpoint in the Iditarod sled dog race, Ophir was a gold mining region in the early part of the twentieth century and long before that, a gold mining region in the Bible. It was named by Bible-toting prospectors for a long lost land, debatably the source of King Solomon's gold (Kings 9:26-28; 10:11,22; 2Chronicles 8: 17-18; 9:1).Beyond Ophir lies the wildest, least populated portion of today's Iditarod trail. Just past Ophir, racers go to the right towards Cripple checkpoint (northern route, even years) or take a left turn and head for Iditarod checkpoint (southern route, odd years). Behind are some easier trails and cozy villages. Ahead, on either route, are long distances, daunting hills, solitude, and often cold—real cold, down to -50° F. When windy as well, you have a recipe for frostbite, drifted-in and obliterated trail, zero visibility, and for becoming lost or stopped dead in your tracks.

From my first race, in 1979, I hark back to kneeling in darkness and into a fierce wind on the frozen Yukon River, then inching forward by using my knife as a piton in the ice, with my lead dog tethered to me by a rope. What was I thinking?! Eventually I had to give up and retreat to a fish camp high on the riverbank to wait out the storm. Such things, and worse, occur with some frequency. *Beyond Ophir*, therefore, one enters what can be the most challenging part of the Iditarod. *Beyond Ophir* symbolizes a leaving behind, a departure from the easy, the comfortable, the secure, the known. It's what we do all our lives—exiting mother's womb, entering grade school, finishing high school, starting careers and families, and ultimately dying. It's what I do each year when I leave home and set out for Nome. Leaving Ophir for what's beyond epitomizes the race's departures, and is my metaphor for life's as well.

Now for a word of explanation regarding this prolog, which I do know how to spell correctly. Ever since lapsing into dog mushing in the 1970s, I have kept a *Dog Log*, a so-titled three ring binder in which I keep not only my kennel records but also the other facts and figures I find relevant to living the good life.

Map Courtesy of Jennifer Thermes.

Table of Contents

Part I

Chapter One
THE RACE

Iditarod Trail Marker and Race Logo

To the uninitiated, let me explain: The Iditarod is a sled dog race in Alaska, from Anchorage to Nome, a distance of approximately 1000 trail miles. It is run by dozens of humans and hundreds of dogs. The start is viewed by thousands of people, and later by no one during countless hours of solo travel and toil. It commences the first weekend in March and ends anywhere from eight to fourteen or more days later as the survivors cross the finish line. It has been dubbed "The Last Great Race on Earth."

The route courses vast tracks of boreal forest, mountains, many rivers, lakes and swamps (mostly frozen) and ocean (variably frozen). Conditions vary from packed snow to deep snow to no snow, and with ice, gravel, rocks, roots and/or tussocks. Temperatures range from -50° F. to + 40° F., and wind is often fierce. Snow can sting the eyes and obscure vision, or when warm or even rainy can soak through to the skin. The country is breathtakingly beautiful but deceptive, in a heartbeat metamorphosing into its hard, cold, punishing alter ego.

At the starting line teams of sixteen (the maximum allowed) eager canines rocket down the trail, their mushers straining to hang on to the sled and keep the show on the road. Spectators are impressed with their speed and power, with all sixteen dogs lined up neatly and pulling for all they're worth. Miles and days later, all this can change as weariness, strained muscles, bad trail and mating instincts combine to take their toll. Carried to the extreme, the whole process can come to resemble the pushing of a noodle of wet spaghetti. But then, the fun has just begun! Those canines get tired and sore, but they are well-fed, watered and bedded-down on straw at each pit stop. Booties are removed, feet lotioned, muscles massaged and, if that is not enough, they are left in the care of veterinarians and at next opportunity are flown back to Anchorage (or later in the race to await you in Nome). The mushers spend most of their checkpoint time performing the above chores, plus repairing equipment and preparing for the next section of trail, without assistance. During these "rests," usually from four to six hours duration, mushers get an hour of sleep, two at most. This continues the entire race, totaling as little as fifteen to twenty hours. Add the miles, the cold, the dark, the injuries, the hallucinations, the broken equipment, the continuous exertion, the wet spaghetti and the urge to quit, and you get considerably strung out. The challenge, then, is to deal with it, to maintain your routine and make decisions under such circumstances. It's not easy, but it can be very rewarding, very accomplishing. It's strange, but I think it's why I struggle through, year after year.

Another Trail Marker, Tripod Type

Chapter Two
OF MICE AND MUSHERS

How did it begin? I mean, how did I begin to be a musher? How did I go to the dogs? It began, like all journeys, with a single step and like this book, with a single stroke of my pen.

Reaching way back to my childhood in Fargo, North Dakota, I was never permitted to have a dog, or any pet. My mother couldn't and wouldn't tolerate an animal in or around her house. That explains a lot, I think, for nowadays my lifestyle entails up to fifty dogs in my kennel, a stone's throw from my house. (Parents, pay heed!)

Circa 1975. For Christmas I gave my kids a newly weaned Siberian husky puppy. We named it "Koaklik," from a Yupik Eskimo word supplied by a dear Alaska Native woman from St. Mary's, Maggie Sipary. Came summer, I attached Koaklik to a bicycle, and the kids' puppy became my puppy as we roamed the bike paths of Anchorage. Little did I know then where that puppy was leading me, like I don't know where I'm going with this book. It's really all *Beyond Ophir*.

When a bicycle with one dog begged for more, I acquired two additional huskies. Winter arrived, and I switched to skis. A dog pulling its human on skis is called skijoring, a popular and reasonable sport. Three dogs pulling is called madness, which I soon discovered. Emboldened by success with one dog, one evening I risked all three of them, and we shot off down the street and onto some trails on the campus of Alaska Pacific University. Right away it hit me that I had bitten off too big a bite. I was a moderately adept skier, but rocketing along at twenty mph in dim light, on the outskirts of control and with no visible means of stopping, other than a crash, was too much. Exciting, though. All I can say is: Don't try it at home! After a couple of those crashes, I terminated the run and concluded that a dogsled loomed large on my horizon.

The dogsled I acquired within a week, from whom or where I don't recollect. Soon I was mushing my three-dog team and was happy, but not for long. I might want to take a trip. So I rounded up more dogs—three more, to be exact. Now, six dogs in front of my sled, surely enough. You can see where this is leading—more dogs, more equipment, longer trips, more dogs.... A more disciplined individual might have been able to rein in the gathering storm.

With reference to equipment, requisite for any musher is the means for transporting your outfit to the local dog track, or to trails out in the countryside. Such transportation comes in the form of a truck and a wooden structure featuring cubbyholes for the dogs—a "dog box," either on the truck bed or towed on a trailer. Initially, I opted for the latter and became acquainted with a guy named Walt Parker, an erstwhile Anchorage musher who had an old trailer with a dog box. If I would haul it away, it was mine. Such a deal! So, one subzero day I dug it out of a snowbank behind Walt's house, towed it to my abode in College Gate subdivision, backed it into our heated garage, and left it there to thaw overnight. Next morning, I awoke to shrieks emanating from the kitchen.

"What's the matter?" I asked my wife.

"They're everywhere—in the cupboards, under the sink...."

That trailer was absolutely crawling with mice, legions of mice, all too happy to abandon trailer and seek residence in a cupboard. Up to that point, my family had been very accepting of my burgeoning addiction, but this was beyond the pale. It came very close to ending my mushing career right then and there. I extracted that dog box from the garage without further ado, and we applied modestly successful pest control. I'm not sure I was ever forgiven, but somehow I was allowed to keep moving on down the trail.

Soon that involved the Kenai Peninsula's Resurrection Trail, thirty-five miles in length, very mountainous, and frequented year round. My trip on that trail began at Hope, on one end, and finished up at Cooper Landing, on the other. At the outset I told my companions—some four or five of them— to load their stuff onto my sled, already laden with gear, too much gear. The idea was that my six dogs and I would speed ahead, reach our first day's destination well before the others, and have the cabin heated and supper cooked when they arrived, on skis. The plan sounded good, but there was a devil in the details: I had not anticipated all the *glaciation*. Where the trail traversed the mountainsides ice had built up, rendering the trip problematic, essentially impossible by my loaded dogsled. The first time I met such obstacle I boldly urged the team forward, only to "glissade" down the mountainside, out of control, dogs scrambling for a claw hold and the sled rolling over two or three times until we came to rest against some trees. By the time I recovered and scrambled back up to the trail, the skiers had caught up with me. They helped me carry all the stuff, and then the dogs and the sled, back up and onto the trail to a point past the ice. I took off, but soon encountered more glaciation. Not eager for another glissade, I waited for the skiers and their aid. This was repeated, time after tiring time until very late and very dark, we all dragged into camp. Everyone was exhausted, and not very happy campers. Three days and a few farces later, we reached the end of the Resurrection. It taught me two things. First, not all trips or trails are suitable for sled dogs, at least not without better equipment and more experience. Second, though misery may love company, your company does not always love misery. It took a few years, but I came to realize that with few exceptions, many people have accompanied me on *one* outing. My companions did not want our Resurrection "resurrected," and they never went anywhere with me again.

Kelly's Lead Dog Contest Trophy

Chapter Three
KELLY

With rare exception, my dogs have been "Alaskan Huskies," a potpourri of village dogs, Siberians, other northern breeds, various types of hounds, and a wayward wolf or two. This mix has evolved over the years into what works well for long distance racing. For the last twenty years I've specialized in *white* Alaskan huskies, and therefore my present "Northern Whites Kennel." More about that later. My rare exception, besides the Siberian puppy, consisted of two Irish Setters. One was dumb as a post, but the other, named "Kelly," had quality canine cognition and was a trained lead dog. Although up in years, he had not slowed much and was a "command leader," meaning he knew right from left, or "gee" from "haw". I obtained Kelly from Shirley Gavin, a locally renowned female musher from Peters Creek, near Anchorage.

In those days, my best mushing buddy was a guy named Ron Gould, a fellow physician I had known during my years of pathology training at the Mayo Clinic. Never short on ideas, Ron talked me into entering Kelly in the Anchorage Fur Rendezvous' Lead Dog Contest. (He later talked me into a great deal more than that.) That lead dog contest consisted of you, your sled, and your lead dog on a barrel-defined slalom course down Anchorage's snow-covered Fourth Avenue. Besides the barrels, there were cars, parking meters, stray dogs and a large crowd of cheering, jeering spectators. Plenty could go wrong, and too bad for Ron, it did. He wound up wrapped around a fire hydrant, a structure altogether too enticing for a dog. Other contestants suffered similar fates. Kelly and I won the thing, a result of the others' misfortune, my *good* fortune and, of course, Kelly! I must confess that to this day, it is the only sled dog race in which I have prevailed, at least as defined by winning. That Setter was the first, but not the worst, in a long line of lead dogs I've had the privilege of owning, over the many years and many miles. Kelly is long dead, but what the hell—long live Kelly!

*Canine Collage. Centered are Kelly (Left) and Dumb as a Post (Right)—
Also Koaklik, the Siberian (to the Rear)*

Chapter Four
INSPIRATION AND SEDUCTION

How many years? How many miles? Now into my thirty-plus year of running sled dogs, I have endured no less than one Iditarod in each of the five calendar decades the race has existed. It makes me one of a very few mushers to have done that. Overall, I have entered and completed sixteen Iditarods, as of March 14, 2013—and counting. I've wanted to pack it in many times, but scratching (quitting) has never been a real option. As to how many miles, my per annum has varied from under 1,000 to more than 3,000. Again as of 2013, that adds up to something like 60,000—more than twice around the Earth at its equator, if you could mush the equator.

I should expand on my beginning. Before that Christmas Siberian, which I gave my kids, came a newspaper. On New Year's Day, 1974, I awoke to an *Anchorage Times* front-page photo of a woman named Judy Gould, wife of my friend, Ron. It showed her on a dog sled, cresting a hill with snow flying and with a joyous, wild, nearly deranged look on her face. Judy had not been a musher when I knew her as a Texan who very reluctantly moved to Alaska. Racing sled dogs would have been at the very bottom of her bucket list. But there she was, appearing downright enraptured. Having followed the Anchorage Fur Rondy races in the sixties but never even *dreaming* I would mush myself, I was both inspired and seduced by the photograph. *If Judy could do that, why not me?*

Judy's fling with the dogsled thing must have been brief because before I knew it, her husband, Ron, had taken over as chief cook and doggie washer in their kennel, and in 1977 he entered the Iditarod. Ron couldn't make it all the way to Nome that year, having floundered and fallen back in a giant snowstorm at mid-race. He was, however, anything but discouraged as he regaled me with tales from the trail, insisting that I must find a way to the Iditarod start myself. On a visit to Anchorage, Ron was accompanied by Dinah Knight, a woman from "Outside" (the Lower 48). Dinah had met up with the same floundering fate as Ron. She was not sure she'd be able to try again and needed to scale back, so she sold me two lead dogs—Grey and Foxie. They didn't cost an arm or leg and were quality critters, so I got a good deal. Armed with those two new leaders and inspired by Ron and Dinah's stories, for the first time I seriously entertained the notion that I just might find my way to that starting line.

Chapter Five
TOLERANCE

"Happy Husky Home," thus christened by my elementary school daughters Margaret and Kim, had swollen to eight furry friends. That's enough to get you into trouble, but not enough for Iditarod. So I wanted more, and I acquired them, one from this kennel, another from that. Buying sled dogs is tricky business. You can get lucky, as with Grey and Foxie, but more often it's like acting on advice from the auctioneer's brother. Mushers always have a dog that is not right for their team, but would fit nicely into yours. Beware—especially if that dog looks like it wants to lean up against something (Mark Twain). Not yet onto all the nuances of dog deals, I soon had animals best described as variable—some that knew gee from haw, and some not. It was not such a bad fit, though, because their new, inexperienced musher could be described the same way.

Our backyard was adorned by pens, ropes and chains, sufficient for its seventeen occupants. I did my best to keep them quiet, and my daughters kept the yard as clean as possible by scooping the poop. (This assured that I need not worry about their growing up to become mushers.) In our subdivision we lived cheek-to-jowl next to multiple neighbors. They were unbelievably tolerant, for which I was very grateful. I must admit, I would not have wanted to live next to me. But as one might predict, even *those* neighbors had a limit. Reaching it, after two years and one Iditarod, one of them knocked on my door. He had been selected as most politically correct by the neighborhood vigilante committee, and he said, "Evening, Jim. The wife allows as how that's quite a herd you've got there." ("The wife," forever a convenient scapegoat.) I replied, "I know. My wife feels the same way (See what I mean?), and we've started searching for a new place." Seemed to satisfy, and a few months later we were gone.

Chapter Six
McGUIRE'S TAVERN

During the winter leading up to the 1978 Iditarod I began touring Tudor Track, since renamed Tozier Track. As Anchorage's official sled dog venue, it is used for sprint racing (short, fast runs), in contrast to long distance. I took my dogs there for a fifteen to twenty-mile outing two or three times each week. On weekends our focus was a junior race, where my daughters would compete against other kids. Margaret got the hang of it, paving the way for a future Junior Iditarod. Sister Kim, on the other hand, had two left paws when it came to mushing. If she didn't fall off the sled, she would take a wrong turn and get lost, paving the way for a future retirement.

My way was paved, in concrete, by a psychiatrist named Vern Stilner who was planning to conduct a study of Iditarod mushers. Vern needed some willing and able assistants to go out on the trail to collect data. I leaped at the chance and took with me a mushing/commercial fishing friend named Steve Davis. A chemist and laboratory technologist, Steve worked with me in the lab at Anchorage's Providence Hospital. He was to obtain and process blood samples from mushers while I administered psychometric tests. The idea was to assess how the race alters contestants' blood counts, body chemistries, thought processes and motor function. I was to document their ability to count serial sevens, tap fingers rapidly, etc. This would entail getting together with each of a selected handful of mushers—prior to the start, at the end, and at points along the way. One of our chosen subjects was soon to be Iditarod champion and legend Dick Mackey, the father of 1983 champion Rick Mackey, of Iditarod veteran Jason Mackey, and of the more recent multi-champ and emerging legend, Lance Mackey.

After the initial session in Anchorage, Steve and I boarded Alaska Airlines for McGrath, a small town and checkpoint about 300 miles into the race. We set up shop in the McGrath health clinic, courtesy of the Alaska Native Health Service. That was our official workplace, but our triage area turned out to be the local watering hole, McGuire's Tavern. Barely into our first beer, or our second, Steve and I were interrupted by an urgent request to return to the clinic. Before our entrance into the tavern, a scuffle had resulted in the exit of a pugilist with a dislocated, fractured thumb. Once people know you're a doc, and the only doc for hundreds of miles, they take you as the man to fix just about anything, so I felt I had to try. For the man's thumb, I rendered my very best pathologist's version of a reduction and splinting, and presently we were back in the bar. Before long another customer required attention, and again to the clinic we went. This continued all day and well into the long, dark Alaskan night. Iditarod in McGrath is party time, particularly so in 1978 when the race was still new. The locals whooped it up big time, as did plenty of not-so-locals. When we came to the end of our tour and exited McGrath, it was on a chartered Medevac flight with me as the flight's physician. On board were eight of my patients. Most spectacular was a woman who had been riding spread-eagle on a sled pulled by her husband's snowmachine (Alaskan for snowmobile). At high speed they ran over a spruce branch protruding from the snow. The branch impaled her where the sun don't shine, after which she paid me a visit. About a hundred spruce needles had to be plucked out of her perineum, something like removing porcupine quills from the muzzle of a dog. A thorough cleansing, many sutures and two hours later, I intimated that she might want to ride the sled in a different position.

Not all were victims of trauma. One guy proved uncommonly interesting, from a medical point of view. Short of breath, he was subsequently diagnosed with a rare lung disease, and a few months later was presented by me at an Alaska Lung Association medical education conference. Another man took a break from his trapline because of headaches. On examination he had severe ("malignant") hypertension with a blood pressure of 210/150 and bleeding in his eyeballs. Having refused the flight to Anchorage for further evaluation, he half listened to my preaching about diet and the medication I prescribed, and then disappeared on his snowmachine to resume his trapping. Doomed, I figured, and correctly because the next time I was in McGrath, that trapper was in a better place. He was just one of those "did it my way" types.

We also observed the emergence of a "do it this new way," though short-lived mushing technique. One musher, named Susan as I recall, announced she had witnessed the solution to tired dogs' not wanting to drink. "You pass this tube down their gullets and pour water into their stomachs." Known as "tubing," it did the job and enjoyed a brief popularity but was banned when race veterinarians pointed out that the water could inadvertently enter the dogs' lungs, causing instead of alleviating a problem.

Besides all the amusement and the practice of my primary profession, we did eventually get around to our mission in McGrath. Nowadays Iditarod racers most often blow right on through McGrath, pausing only five or ten minutes, if that; but in those early days most would happily linger there for a few hours, or longer. That's when Steve and I were able to spend some time with our subjects, squeezed in amongst the sick, the injured, the good, the bad and the ugly. Further down the trail, in Unalakleet and lastly Nome, we accomplished get-togethers with each one of our half-dozen-or-so racers. To no one's surprise, their ability to count sevens and tap fingers, etc. as above, did not improve. Dr. Stilner massaged the data and published it in a medical journal. I don't know if it proved much, but I do know that the whole musher study thing further strengthened my resolve to run the big race.

Chapter Seven
SOMETHING FISHY

The next summer passed doglessly, in terms of running the dogs. Such a time-off period has been my norm for real recuperation and the healing of any injuries, including the undetected, after the long, strenuous winter. At the onset of Alaskan autumn, in late August, I kicked off the season with a moose/caribou hunt. I'm referring to the *mushing* season because my hunting friends and I went sled dog hunting—not hunting sled dogs, but hunting *with* sled dogs. Our hunting/camping equipment piled high on a gutted Volkswagen chassis, we had the dogs pull it on an old mining road into a non-motorized hunting area north of the Denali Highway. Each morning we headed out bright and early, shot an animal, and trudged back to camp to fetch the dogs. They then pulled a sled across the tundra to the kill site and, with meat piled on the sled, pulled it back to our camp. An efficient way to hunt and a strenuous workout for all, it was a great way to start fall training. Additionally, at night and in theory, it was a great way to know if a grizzly bear was near because a canine chorus would give us plenty of warning. Trouble was, the dogs gave us that warning about every ten minutes, bear or no bear. Already concerned about bear attraction with fresh meat hanging and a bitch (female dog) in heat, it kept us on edge, and awake. On the upside, it was valuable training for the sleep-depriving Iditarod.

Gutted

Back to camp

On the subject of sleep deprivation, another such insomnious activity received my attention during summertime. It was commercial salmon fishing, and it relates to mushing because sled dogs love to eat fish and because many mushers were at least part-time commercial fishermen. I was no exception, and I plied the waters of Northern Cook Inlet each July, in pursuit of the slimy sockeye (red salmon). As a multifamily cooperative, we loaded fishing nets and other gear, food, kids and a dog or two into our boats and sailed to our fish camp near the mouth of the Big Susitna River (therefore, our "Su Fish Company"). Much of the time we lazed around, awaiting the next "opening," a period of time designated by Alaska Fish and Game as "open" for fishing. With frequent nice weather (by Alaskan standards), water holes for swimming, muddy banks for sliding, and tall grass as far as the eye could see, it was a children's paradise. While the kids played, the adults mended nets and otherwise readied for the next fishing period. Consistently greedy for more salmon, I often stayed up, *dreaming* up new and admittedly screwy ways of doing things. One of the screwiest was an elaborate system of ropes and pulleys, which we established from the shore out onto the mud at low tide. Again in theory, it would enable us to deploy our nets from land, in case heavy seas prevented us from using our boats. Unproven theory it remains, sadly, since the one time we tried it a few flaws interfered, e.g. seaweed clogging the pulleys. Nevertheless, this "system" did do something: It earned us a moniker, "The Rope People," as coined by the Redingtons, the illustrious mushing clan whose "wish" site was not far from ours.

Su Fish, at Fish Camp
Photo Courtesy of Steve and Rachel Harrison, Willow, Alaska

Came the next opening, we set our nets, picked out the fish, retrieved the nets, reset them, picked them... It was grimy, toilsome and even dangerous from time to time, as in the reputation of commercial fishing. Tides in the Anchorage area are the second highest in the world, sometimes forty feet from low to high. Water moves as a raging torrent that, combined with strong wind from a glacier, can with little warning create extremely hazardous boating conditions. More than one time we ran for our lives, desperately seeking calmer water before our luck ran out, as it once did for another party in our area. During that episode we had just wrapped up our fishing at "outer nets," the low tide location about two miles out to sea from the (high tide) shore. At first calm but cloudy—and even sultry—a stiff breeze arose from Turnagain Arm, an ocean fjord so-named by Captain Cook eons ago. With tidal current raging and waves mounting, we frantically pulled in our six 200-foot, fish-filled nets—sticks, scales, gills, guts, feathers and all. We barely got it into our two boats before it was undoable in the surging seas. Though our camp was not far away, returning to its safe haven was not an option since it would entail porpoising perilously downwind in the now five to six-foot waves, with three thousand pounds of salmon on board. So we motored directly *into* the waves, putting us on a slow, twenty-mile course to shelter with steadily worsening conditions. For an hour we pounded through the turbulent, silty-grey sea, its chilling spray dousing me continually at the aft-ward helm of *The Hooley*, my twenty-five-foot open skiff. My friends and fishing partners, Steve Davis and the Harrisons, set sail near to us but diverged beyond any comforting field of vision as they battled the elements on a nearly parallel but parting route. And then, just as we were nearing calmer water, disaster damned near struck. Immediately afore was a rogue wave, a monstrous water wall stretching to port and starboard as far as we could see. It left no option but to steer straight for it. This was many years before *Perfect Storm*, or I would have recognized it as *Perfect Wave*, an untimely convergence of wind and tide. When we hit it, it hit us, wrenching my skiff sideways, and we came close to capsizing as I strove mightily to regain control. Then we made it through and reunited with our friends. They told us about their similarly terrifying moments with the rogue, and we all vowed to stay ashore, until the next opening.

Sleep deprivation was an integral part of the commercial fishing game, and a game it was, for me. There was the time we had just finished "playing" an exceptionally long game and were all dog tired, when I relayed a radio message to my crew that "It's open, *indefinitely.*" Exhausted, my kids literally fell over onto a big pile of smelly sockeyes, as they were then committed to one more day and night of toil and turmoil, not to mention the smell and the slime. Where were the child labor laws when they needed them?

The Author and The Hooley, out onto the Mud (aka shallow sea fishing)
Photo Courtesy of Steve and Rachel Harrison, Willow, Alaska

Another time, in a span of twenty-four hours and due to the usual comedies of errors, my skiff sank—not once but twice. On each sinking it went completely underwater and with the same outboard engine, so we lost another night's sleep but only *one* ruined engine. Now there's a silver lining for you!

Yet another time, under unusual regulatory circumstances, we were tied to a set net salmon beach for six days of continuous forced labor, catching only two hours sleep per tide, only four hours per day. Why did we do all that stuff? Being commercial fishing, it was officially for the money obtained by selling the salmon, and in a good year there could be enough, after expenses, to apply a few dollars toward impending college tuitions. But truth be told, money had little to do with it. First, there was seldom very *much* money, and second, we were out there because we (some of us, anyway) loved it. The lifestyle, the dreaming and scheming on how to optimize the catch, the work and long hours, the sea breezes and yes, even the danger. Why is this so? It's something akin to why people climb mountains, the "because it's there" thing—and for sure, I repeat, it's why I struggle through Iditarod, year after year.

Chapter Eight
THE ROUTINE

At some point late that fall of 1978, or early winter, I did two things. For one thing, I signed up for the 1979 race. For races subsequent to the Iditarod's first decade, signing up has required a demanding qualification, with successful completion of hundreds of miles of other, shorter races. In 1979 the only qualification was the successful ponying-up of your entry fee of $1049 (now a few times that amount). You needed never have run in *any* races, which was exactly my situation. My first Iditarod was my first sled dog race of any kind. Talk about green, I was its definition. What a learning experience, but I'm ahead of my story.

So, for another thing, at first snowfall I initiated the training and conditioning of my team. Nowadays all that starts earlier, around Labor Day, with short daytrips in warm weather and using a four-wheeler (ATV). The dogs pull the machine, same as they pull a sled. I clarify that because without the clarification, on one occasion someone came away with a both erroneous and humorous image of the dogs being pulled *behind* the four-wheeler. Believe me, such *pulling* of the wet noodle would be a mess. Anyway, at that time mushers were not training with four-wheelers and besides, I didn't have one. They may not have even been invented.

From Halloween to early January my training runs were all at Anchorage's Tudor track, the short and easy runs to which I have already alluded. Some days I would pull off back-to-back runs, adding up to some thirty or even forty miles. It was still a powder-puff deal for the dogs, with too easy pulling on groomed racing trails. I later learned that the dogs should be conditioned by putting more weight in the sled, such as bags of sand or dog food, or a person. Another technique is towing a large, heavy tire (and another is a four-wheeler). Blissfully ignorant of my shortcomings, I carried on with my quest.

The two to four hour run times were just the beginning. Loading equipment and dogs into my truck and trailer, driving to the track, and unloading and hooking up the team required about two hours. After the run, the reverse procedure added another two, so the whole affair was a six to eight hour proposition. Commencing in the evening, after a full day's work as a pathologist, it made for some very late nights, and tired next days. Looking back on it, I don't know how I managed. Younger and foolisher, I guess.

It might sound as if we routinely whizzed around the course, free of any trouble. To the contrary, the "whizzing" was seldom routine or trouble-free. To make my point, I offer the examples below.

Always open to some variety, I took a detour by leaving the designated sled dog trails and venturing up the Anchorage Hillside to a restaurant called Stuckagain Heights. Bursting out of the woods and into Stuckagain's parking lot, I succeeded in turning the team around without banging into more than one or two of the parked cars. My only mistake was taking my eyes off some of the team members, as I fed the others a small snack. This was plenty of time for one of the males to mount a female in heat. Not desiring a delayed departure, nor an unplanned pregnancy, I reflexively brought the back of my hand down just as the dogs were rising up. When hand struck head I felt both a pop and a pain, suffering a musher's version of a boxer's fracture. Having successfully but stupidly avoided a mating, we bolted out of that parking lot and down the mountainside. Now, mushing down a mountain is never easy, though often thrilling. That time it was one of those hang-on-for-dear-life deals, with one hand. The fractured hand, stuffed into my large mushing mitt, was puffed up like a toad and hanging useless. By the hardest, we made it to my truck, after which I got to a payphone and called my daughters for help.

Perhaps it was my immobilized right hand that compelled my wife to have a go at mushing, and one evening she took out a team at that same Tudor Track. Even greener than I, she failed to return to the truck by the expected time. After an extensive ground search, I wound up placing a 911 call. Located by a police helicopter, the team was high on the Anchorage Hillside and wrapped around a tree, without wife. Hours earlier she had been flipped on her back, got torn up when dragged through some bushes, and had lost the team. After walking for miles without finding the dogs, she made it to a road and flagged down an automobile. The driver about dropped his jaw when he saw her, covered with blood. I'm sure he feared she was the victim of some assault and was relieved to hear it was just the result of another day's mushing misadventure.

Chapter Nine
A TRUE STORY

My Iditarods have required many months of preparation, with one exception. The exception occurred in 1984 when before the race and while at work at the hospital, I received a visitor. That visitor was none other than the noted musher and adventurer, Norman Vaughan. One could write a whole book or two about Norman, as he did. Suffice to say that Col. Norman Vaughan, World War II allied sled dog commander, mushing Olympian, Antarctic dog musher with Admiral Byrd, and an Iditarod veteran, was my good friend and godfather to my son Jimmy. On the visit at the hospital he sat beside me over coffee and said, "Jim, I'm sick, and I want you to take my team in the Iditarod." His sickness was not serious, but his proposal was, and I agreed to it.

With less than a month until the race, I ran his dogs a few times and assembled my gear. Early one frosty morning Norman appeared on my doorstep and asked if I needed anything. I told him yes, and I also asked if *he* needed anything, like breakfast. I knew that offer would not be long refused since Norman was a notoriously voracious eater, right up to his 100th birthday party. Our conversation at an end and Norman hungry as usual, he took off in my truck to fetch some items at a store.

Now, a few days earlier my old lead dog, Foxie, had passed away. Foxie's cremated remains I had laid on the passenger seat of my truck, in a transparent plastic bag. Upon his return from the store, Norman stood in my doorway, the opened plastic bag in hand, and said, "Jim, this is mighty lousy trail food you've got here!" And that's the true story of how Norman Vaughan ate my lead dog.

Foxie, for Breakfast

Chapter Ten
CLEAR AND COLD

In the years since 1979 I have prepared for each Iditarod by taking part in one or more mid-distance races, each anywhere from 150 to 400 miles in length. Race names include the Sheep Mountain, the Knik 200, the Klondike, the Northern Lights, the Don Bowers, the Tustumena 200, the Copper Basin 300, the Kusko 300, the Gold Foot, the Taiga, the Gin Gin, the Denali Double, and the All Alaska Sweepstakes. My only race outside Alaska is the 1996 Hope Race, an 800-mile adventure in the Chukotka region of the Russian Far East. Some of these I've raced more than once. Since many of them are memorable, I will undoubtedly have occasion to refer to their haps and mishaps, someday.

As I have mentioned, the 1979 Iditarod was my very first race, so it was not preceded by any of the above mid-distancers. It was preceded by excursions such as in January of that year when I drove my dogs and equipment the 300 or so miles clear up to Clear, the Alaskan community where my friend Ron Gould lived. That took me into the Interior, the large central region of Alaska where winter temperatures are colder than in South Central, where I live and do most of my training. As I traveled north of McKinley National Park (since renamed Denali) my truck's heater was struggling to keep me warm and keep the windshield free of frost. A few miles past the town of Healy the highway descended onto a broad, flat and very cold plain. At this point, the entire windshield went "chink," suddenly freezing over into nearly impenetrable ice. I couldn't see a thing. Ron's place was no more than 50 miles away, but it required four or five hours to get there as I crept along, peering through a three inch hole kept open by constant scraping with a plastic card. Finally at my destination and grateful I hadn't frozen to death, I spent the better part of an hour lying with Ron on the ground under my vehicle's engine. We made modifications he said were crucial for the cold; and cold it was, -65° F.

We tethered my dogs amidst a grove of scrawny trees. Thanks to a recent storm, the snow was deep, providing insulating burrows for the animals. Nestled down in its burrow atop some dry straw, each dog rolled up into its very snug little ball of fur. It's impressive how huskies can tolerate such temperatures and even thrive, provided they are given plenty of quality food to pay back the lost calories.

In the midst of that severe cold, Iditarod champ Jerry (Gerald) Riley drove over from nearby Nenana. Jerry, known as "Wolverine Riley," was widely respected as one of the toughest and most skilled woodsmen in Alaska. He said to me, "Come outside, Jim, and I'll show you how to start a fire at 65 below." Such skill could come in handy in the Iditarod, even life-saving, so I fell in and followed. Standing among those scrawny trees, Jerry whacked one with his ax and whittled its end into a woodsman's fleurs-de-lys. "Now watch," he boasted, "One match." Nearly an hour, two or three "fleurs-de-lyses" and many matches later, the great Wolverine Riley muttered something about wet wood as we beat a frigid retreat to Ron's house, sans fire.

The Gentler Side of a Wolverine, Reading to my Son Willy

For most of that severe cold spell, which lasted several more days, we hunkered down inside. My family had come up from Anchorage, and my kids joined Ron's in playing a video game, Pacman, a brand-new craze at that time. Ron and I tried running the dogs in the "heat" of the day—around -55°. The initial plunge, zipping along at more than twenty miles per hour, was so painful to any little bit of exposed skin that we aborted the run and rejoined the video game.

Finally, on about the fourth day, the weather warmed up to -40°. Believe it or not, it felt almost balmy, and we went out for a tolerable two or three hours. Ten days earlier, Ron had again visited me in Anchorage, and we had trained together. At that time, his team was faster than my (slow) team. In the interim I had acquired four new dogs from a musher named Duke Bertke, long since retired from mushing. That acquisition proved beneficial, and in the cold at Clear I moved faster than Ron. This speed differential persisted to and through the '79 Iditarod, and it helped me keep up with my friend. It also demonstrated, not surprisingly, what a positive influence a few new dogs can have on a team.

A few days passed with daily runs but no warming of the -40°. Receiving rumor of warmer temperatures to the south, I Cleared out, with Ron's brother-in-law, to Cantwell, Alaska, and a toasty -10° or so. We started out with two teams, eastbound on the snow-covered Denali Highway. The weather was calm at first, but at about 25 miles we ran into a north wind. We turned around into both increasing wind and falling temperature and were caught in a ground blizzard fiercer than anything I had weathered up to that point in my mushing career. Almost unable to see our lead dogs, after three or four hours we made it back to my truck and kissed the gravel on which it was parked. Not fun, but it would prove advantageous, yet again readying me for the approaching Iditarod.

Chapter Eleven
KISS

February found me drawing near to the food drop date, the day dog food and other supplies for each checkpoint must be ready for delivery to a warehouse in Anchorage. After cutting up meat and fish, the musher apportions it into small bags, along with kibble, fat, vitamins, medications, human food and other items as desired. Then all that is dumped into large "drop bags" provided by the Iditarod Trail Committee—three per checkpoint, as a rule. The whole shebang fills the eight-foot bed of a pickup truck and totals 1500 pounds or more, when weighed by volunteers at the warehouse.

Preparing the food drop is a huge undertaking, in spades the first time, for a race rookie. A cardinal rule, for the drops and for every aspect of Iditarod, is KISS. Keep It Simple, Stupid. Most rookies don't do that, and I didn't do that. Consequently, preparing the drop was huger than it should have been.

For example, having received some sheefish from Northwest Alaska, I thawed them and processed each one by filleting and skinning, as for human consumption. All that's required, and much faster, is to dice 'em up with a ban saw. I filleted those fish at my garage sink while some family friends, the Coyles, were working over a bunch of beavers given to me by a trapper. When the Coyles arrived I introduced them to the beavers, strewn on the garage floor. The dead, skinned, partially frozen rodents with their large, rat-like heads and teeth were reminiscent of some old fashioned horror movie. It required some adjustment to get on with the task at hand. Eventually, armed with an ax, a hand saw and a butcher knife, they commenced an arduous, prolonged dissection of all those cold cadavers. When the butcher knife was driven into the flesh and twisted, its business end broke off and remained in the beaver. That knife still resides in a kitchen drawer and goes on and on—without end, so to speak. As per my instructions, my friends "boned out" the beavers, resulting in pieces of pure meat, like roasts and filet mignons. As with the sheefish, dogs can consume beaver undissected, bones and all. So again, simply axing them into pieces would have sufficed and been much more efficient.

Like many guys new to mushing, I got to know Joe Redington, Sr., the Father of the Iditarod. What old Joe didn't know about mushing wasn't known about mushing. One thing he knew was honey balls, which he fed to his dogs all along the trail from Anchorage to Nome. His honey balls were a mixture of hamburger meat, corn oil, rice, eggs, wheat germ, vitamins, and the honey. It might surprise a person, but dogs really like that stuff. Therefore, I purchased the ingredients and mixed a large quantity of them into a garbage can. Then my daughters laboriously fashioned the "balls" like fat little hamburger patties, plopped them down on a sheet of plywood, and lugged the whole thing outside to freeze.

In recent years I've resurrected the honey balls in a new and less time consuming version, but early in my mushing career I did everything the hard way. That hard way, I must confess, was often the fun way. Creating and experimenting each mushing season, I found myself always trying new ways of doing things. Some of the innovations proved beneficial, like those already tested by another musher. Many did not, like the ones I dreamed up and tried for the first time at the Iditarod starting line, or miles later. Mistake there, but I couldn't help myself, even though I knew I'd be more competitive if I could resist.

Consider my "gangline extenders". Originally suggested to me by Rick Swenson during a tete-a-tete at Skwentna, they *extend* your gangline, make it longer, and thus increase the distance between each pair of dogs by about a foot. Once more in theory, each dog, accustomed to being some five feet to the rear of the rear in front of him/her, would respond to an increase to six feet by attempting to narrow the gap, and therefore pull harder, resulting in the whole team moving faster. The first, and last, time I actually applied this technology was years later at the Cripple checkpoint, where I installed the extenders and explained them to Swenson and Susan Butcher. "Rick," I said, "Do you remember telling me about them at Skwentna?" to which Rick replied, "What was I drinking?" Susan may have been more impressed because two days later, on the Yukon River, she asked, with apparent sincerity, "How are those extenders working, Jim?" I told her, "I don't know. I was moving well before, and I'm moving well now." Without a control group, how *could* I know? So much for the extenders. Another theory they remain.

Another "innovation" was more of a carrot in front of the horse. One day Anna, my wife, spied me in our kennel, standing on a large tarp and holding a female dog in heat. "What the devil are you doing?!" she asked, and I answered, "Trying to collect some dog piss." I succeeded and froze up some aliquots of the bitch's urine, no doubt reeking with hormones. Sled dogs, males in particular as one would expect, run faster when chasing a female in season, so I imagined that some sexy urine might simulate. Part way through next season's Iditarod I drowned a dog bootie in the stuff and tied it to the front of the gangline. It produced no noticeable effect, but it provided a diversion from what might have been a dull day. No noticeable effect, but it gave Anna an idea. Preparing for the next year's race, I asked her to place a few spoonfuls of Tang, my favorite trail drink, into small Ziploc bags. Three weeks later, inside at a checkpoint, I was dispensing the contents of one of those bags into a thermos when another musher asked, "What's written on that stuff, Jim?" Anna, desiring to both energize me and provide some entertainment, had labeled the bags "Viagra".

In counterbalance to my unsuccessful innovations, mistakes and stupidities, I am pardonably adept at delegating, taking a lesson from Tom Sawyer and his whitewashed fence. Let me give a great big thank you hug to all the friends, family, benefactors, delegatees and others who have helped me over the years.

Chapter Twelve
ONE SNOWMACHINE

Accomplishing the February food drop leaves about three weeks to make final preparations for the first Saturday in March, the Iditarod's annual kickoff day. This consists of equipment alterations, shipping backup sleds to checkpoints like McGrath and Unalakleet, veterinary examinations, electrocardiograms and blood tests on each dog, and final runs. These runs have customarily been relatively short, on the order of twenty to forty miles, though longer in recent years as the approach to training and racing has evolved. Three hundred fifty miles by snowmachine over some of the roughest terrain in the Iditarod is not commonly on the agenda, not any time and certainly not just a few days before race start. One time, however, that's exactly what happened—or might have happened.

In year 2000, Anna was set to tackle her first Iditarod, as the first Russian woman in the Last Great Race. I thought it would benefit her to see the first, and the roughest, third of the course, from the start to McGrath. Just one week prior to race day, and less than that before a mandatory mushers' meeting, Anna and I took off by snowmachine—*one* snowmachine. Out of Knik and on the way to the Susitna River, we passed two mushing friends, Robert Bundtzen and Zack Steer, who were on a tune-up run. They must have wondered what we were doing out there, without our dogs, on our one snowmachine. I should have wondered too.

Then up the Yentna River, on past the Yentna and Skwentna checkpoints, through forest and upon swamps, the 150 miles to Finger Lake was smooth sailing. There we took pleasure in the company of Carl and Kirsten Dixon at their Wintersong Lodge, site of the Finger Lake checkpoint. Leaving Finger, Anna could visualize what "the roughest" meant with Happy River's switchbacks, sudden downhills, steep uphills, aggravating sidehills and sharp turns, punctuated by inconveniently situated trees you hope to miss.

Thirty bumpy miles later we stopped briefly at Rainy Pass Lodge on Puntilla Lake, site of the Rainy Pass checkpoint. By that time the weather had begun to deteriorate with increasing clouds, snow and wind. Informed that the trail past Puntilla had been marked, we left the lodge and bravely but naively headed up into the high, open country approaching Rainy Pass, the narrow gap in the Alaska Range through which mushers must "pass" on their way to Rohn. After a few hours and a pointless survey of a false valley, we misread the trail and the few markers and unknowingly started up in the direction of Hell's Gate and Ptarmigan Pass, the wrong pass, the one traversed two weeks earlier by the Iron Dog snowmachine race. Many miles longer than via Rainy and featuring lots of open water on the South Fork of the Kuskokwim River, that route to Rohn has not been used for the Iditarod since the race's earliest years. By this time the snow was heavy and horizontal, reducing visibility to near zero. The route ahead further obscured by the gathering gloom of night, it was time to admit I didn't have the faintest notion where we were headed, and I turned around with intention to beat it back to Puntilla. Too eager to get out of there and navigating mostly by intuition, I skidded onto thin ice above a beaver dam, and we broke right through. Unable to extract the snowmachine but in possession of our supplies, on a sled bolted to the machine's rear end, we changed into some dry clothes and made camp for the night. So far, so bad, but things got worse, as I came down with a sickness and lay in the tent, weak and nauseated. At least we *had* a tent, also dry sleeping bags, some food, and a backpacking stove to melt snow for drinking water. One thing we did *not* have was another snowmachine (I had kept it simple, stupid!), but another thing we *did* have was a brand-new emergency locator beacon, which I had given Anna for her race. Feeling rotten and knowing we were in some degree of trouble, I turned it on, having no idea if it was working, or what might happen if it *did* work.

By next morning the wind and heavy snowfall had abated, but we were still enveloped by thick clouds, or fog. We awoke to the sound of an airplane high overhead, but then lower and closer as it made a few passes over our position. With our noses poked out the tent door, we beheld an awesome sight. Materializing magically from out of the grayness was a

CI30, the four-engine transport of the US military. Looming large and black, it reminded me of Darth Vader as it swept by. On about a third pass, from very low and directly over us, it dropped a small parachute, which landed a meager snowball's throw away. Anna fetched it through deep precipitation and read its message aloud. "If you are in real distress, wave your arms vigorously. If not, turn off that (damn) beacon!" To me, sick and concerned for our safety, this was a no-brainer, but Anna saw things differently. She said, "We're not in danger of dying (yet), so not in real distress (yet). Jim, turn that thing off!" Now, a man cannot reliably predict a woman, and can only begin to understand one. I didn't expect Anna's reaction and can only guess what possessed her. Perhaps her Darth Vader was a Soviet Big Brother, a disguised KGB agent bent on hauling her off to the Gulag. Any guessing aside, she persisted with "Turn it off!" and in my weakened condition, I complied.

After the rumble of the plane faded into distant mountains, the silence became deafening. Any novelty associated with our situation wore off, and we idled through an uninspired yet reasonably comfortable day. By nightfall I felt better, and we made plans to leave the next morning. Only a handful of food was left, and we had exhausted the white gas for melting snow. (What's more, our small flask of brandy was dispiritingly empty.)

Came the dawn. Taking with us only what we deemed practical and necessary for survival, we set off down the valley—on foot. On foot, *as opposed to on snowshoes*. The stupidity of only one snowmachine was exceeded only by our taking *no* snowshoes. Never before had I done anything so dumb as to venture into the Alaskan winter wilderness with no snowshoes, and now we paid the price. The snow was deep and soft, and we sank in up to our waists. Anna surmised that our dogs travel on all fours for a reason. On hands and knees, we sank less and progressed a little faster as we crawled, and pulled our supply bags.

Thus deployed, we inched along with Anna in the fore and me lagging behind, which she charitably attributed to my sickness. Soon our canteens were drained dry, and the midday sun beat down mercilessly. In the face of knowing better, the urge to eat snow having grown irresistible, we ate but only became thirstier and tireder, as well as convinced we had no chance of making the twenty miles to Puntilla and the lodge. Crawling like turtles and moving like snails, by late afternoon we had covered only about three of those miles. I knew of an emergency shelter cabin about halfway, but it was not sighted, and we knew the night would be cold—

subzero. Out of food and water, without tent and without cabin, we would need to dig a snow cave to stay alive.

Why we had not considered turning the locator beacon back on I don't know, but it wasn't necessary, for at that rather low point a large military helicopter came coptering up the valley, heading our way. Now we *did* wave our arms, vigorously, but the helicopter flew on by, without any indication it had seen us. It did, however, proceed up the valley and go down in the general location of our campsite. Not long afterward, it reappeared, made a beeline for us as it traced our tracks, and landed close by. After we hustled the short distance to the craft, its crew didn't need to ask twice if we'd like a lift. That crew consisted of about eight Air National Guardsmen, weekend warriors out on search and rescue detail, following up on Darth Vader. As soon as we were airborne, a navigator type turned to us and said, "You guys all right, and where would you like to go?" I replied, "No worries, mate, and how about

Sign We Posted on a Trail Marker, Later Returned to Us by the Helicopter Crew

Providence Hospital?" That may have suggested we *did* have worries, but I chose the hospital because it was where I worked and had left my truck, and because I knew it had a helipad.

En route we picked up a contestant in the Iditaski race, an Italian guy who had said "Ciao" to his competition when he became inundated by deep snowfall. He spoke just enough English to indicate he was exceedingly happy to see us. Shortly after taking on the Italian we flew to a grand finale. Rendezvousing with a large aircraft, possibly another CI30, we witnessed a midair refueling of the helicopter. We were told it was exceptional for civilians to see such a thing, even against regulations. So what else was new? The entire escapade had been irregular.

Upon landing at Providence, we were met not only by medical personnel but also by the Anchorage police. My daughters had gotten word of my mischief and had tipped off officialdom. After both medical and quasi-criminal interrogations, we were released. Next morning Anna showed up for the musher meeting as if nothing had happened.

Chapter Thirteen
THE LAST SUPPER

At that meeting—always on a Thursday—race officials, sponsors and volunteers are introduced. The race marshal reviews the rules and the trail conditions, and the chief vet counsels on considerations having to do with dog care. Pointed questions and thorny issues often prompt solemn discussions, which eventuate in answers and rule interpretations by the race authorities, sometimes requiring the wisdom of Ophir's King Solomon. It's all in closed session, off limits to the public and the press, for good reason. The entertainment is interrupted by a lunch break, beginning with a champagne toast and a posed photo of all the mushers. (I've often wondered what happens to the photographs since I've never seen a one of them.) Then, during the modern-day Thursday meetings, each musher meets his/her "rider," a sports fan who prevailed in a sealed bid auction to ride in the musher's sled the first day of the race. It's great fun for the winning bidder, the musher and the spectators, and the proceeds support the Iditarod. For several years my rider has been a Bostonian named Charlie Dumbaugh, who has fanned the Red Sox fever of my son, Jimmy.

2012 Rider Charlie and Team Northern Whites, at a Snowy Race Start on Anchorage's Fourth Avenue.
Photo Courtesy of Louis Le, www.Go2Moon.com

The evening of that same day finds everyone at the pre-race banquet. For the most part, this affair has occurred at spacious spots like the Sullivan Arena and the Dena'ina Center, where Anna, Jimmy and I have some years sung our National Anthem and the Alaska State Song. The evening's main event is the mushers' drawing of their starting bib numbers. In 1979 the banquet was held at a smaller venue, a ballroom at the Hilton Hotel. It's funny how certain seemingly insignificant things stick in your memory. The thing I remember about that event is entering the ballroom just behind Rick Swenson, the (now) five-time race winner who had won in 1977 and had lost to Dick Mackey in 1978—by one second. I was struck by his swagger, which fit the reputation he had accrued, and cultivated? He entered that ballroom and the race like a young lion, definitely the man to beat and daring anyone to try. He appeared to possess the confidence that he could win, that he *expected* to win. That confident air can be noted in many of the race's winners. I didn't have it in 1979. Truth is, I've never had it, and I've never won, or even come close. Maybe next year.

The banquet features a tasty meal, sort of a last supper. That makes next day a Good Friday, a good day for last minute repair and rearrangement of equipment, if not dogs. A rookie, like rookie Jim Lanier in '79, rearranges about every fifteen minutes, bouncing from one poor plan to an even poorer one. By nightfall there's still unfinished business, so the rookie is in his garage, going at it till midnight or later. May as well, because when he does go to bed his mind is already racing, and sleep doesn't come. As a result, by race's start he's exhausted.

In the countdown to my first Iditarod, Ron Gould and team were billeted at my domicile in Anchorage. Ron was less ready than I, but with a relaxed, astonishingly nonchalant attitude. By Friday midnight he had not even begun working on his lines. Sounds like an actor procrastinating on his approach to a play. To a musher, lines are the ropes in front of the sled to which the dogs are attached. Ron stayed up all night and was putting on finishing touches at the start. Other teams were hooked-up, barking to go, and Ron sat on the snow, braiding ropes, without a care in the world. That was one difference between Ron and me. While both of us lost sleep, I was less than ready, and worried. Ron knew he was nowhere near prepared, but he didn't seem to give a damn. During that race, and in years before and after, he never looked worried, or in a rush to do anything. Enviable, no?

The Great Gould

Part II

Chapter Fourteen
BEGINNINGS

The prior narrative has led up to the actual running of 1979's Iditarod VII. I could say the same thing about the first four decades of my life, and I might speculate about the decades to come. What is not speculation is that my first race was, and still is, the most memorable of all my Iditarods. I've heard the same thing said by a number of race veterans. That first trip to Nome will serve as a framework for the rest of my tale.

Which year the Iditarod joined the Fur Rendezvous race by starting on Anchorage's Fourth Avenue, I don't remember. In 1979 it started at Mulcahy Stadium, as in 1974. I know that because I was there in 1974, not as a musher but as a spectator. At that time I observed numerous notables whose names reverberate in the annals of mushing: Carl Huntington (the eventual race Champion), Herbie Nayokpuk (The Shishmaref Cannonball), Rudy Demoski Sr., Dan Seavey (sire/grandsire of all them other Seaveys), Ron Aldrich, Bud Smyth (father of Ramey and Cim), Tom Mercer, Robert Ivan, Tim White, Mary Shields and Lolly Medley (the first women to finish the Iditarod), Joel Kottke, Red Fox Olson, John Ace, George Attla (legendary sprint musher), Isaac Okleasik, Jerry Riley, Jack Schultheis, Bill Vaudrin, Bernie Willis, Rod Perry, Howard Farley, Dave Olson, Slim Randles, Dick Mackie, Terry Adkins, Darrel Reynolds, Victor Kotongan, Ken Chase, Joee and Raymie Redington, and Joe Redington Sr. (Father of the Iditarod, and of Joee and Raymie) – to name a few.

Everything was big—big dogs, big teams, big sleds, big dreams. Only the second Iditarod, and those dog drivers were just beginning to figure out how to do it. Smaller and faster dogs, smaller sleds with lighter loads, more efficient technique, scientifically produced dog food, practical dog booties, intensive veterinary care, a well-established and well-marked trail—all that would come later. By 1979 incremental improvements had occurred, but by today's standards the race was still primitive.

I woke up that mornin' just a-barely in time,
I leaped in my truck and I drove to the line,
Loaded sixteen dogs,
Said goodbye to my home,
Then I pulled the hook, and we headed for Nome....
— T. E. FORD, plagiaristically

A memory so acute, it's like the present.

My Crew at the Race Start, 1979

Accompanied and aided by family and friends, and with hundreds of curious spectators spectating, I pull the hook (a metal device by which the sled is anchored to the snow) and we spring ahead, or *around* the stadium's oval track. In the sled is my rider de rigueur, not the paying race patron of later years but a friend, Elliott Barske. Elliott has helped me train my team, and in that team is one of his dogs, named Preacher. Led by Dinah Knight's Foxie and Gray, Preacher and the others in my thirteen-dog outfit pull Elliott and me for several miles along bicycle and cross-country ski trails, then along the Tudor Track sled dog trails. We gain the "wilds" of Muldoon, an Anchorage neighborhood, where in 1984 my race will nearly come to a very premature termination when I stop the team to sort out a few dogs. In the process one of them gets loose, scoots off down the trail, and disappears around the next bend. The near termination involves a race rule specifying that a team cannot continue without all dogs accounted. If my dog were to turn off the trail into someone's backyard, I might not reclaim it for hours, or even days. My race, barely begun, would be over. Not for the last time, however, the mushing gods are smiling on me. After about a mile, there's my dog, tied to a tree. Jerry Austin, a well-known and well-liked musher from St. Michael, was running further on down the trail. He caught my loose animal and secured it. Whew!

The Starting Line

So Fast, I'm Just a Blur

In the Wilds of Muldoon

Another near termination will befall me in 2002 when, again on that ceremonial first day and pulling Anna in back of me on the "whip" sled, I narrowly miss crashing into a large tree on a tight turn. Anna is not as fortunate and *does* crash, jerking the dogs, my sled and me to a sudden halt, whereupon I am even less fortunate as I soar over the sled's handlebar and eat snow. Snagged in the soaring, my left groin pains me some, but I pay no heed, and we finish the run. About an hour later I stop in at the Providence Hospital emergency room where examination reveals fat and other tissue poking out of a three-inch gash. After the suturing and application of a dressing, a nurse pontificates that I must avoid any strenuous activity for the next week, like the Iditarod? Sure. A short time later, the dressing is coming undone, so I redo it. No, I *over*do it. I encase my entire pelvis in an Alaskan's best friend— duct tape. Thus adorned, with my new "dressing" about as comfortable as a medieval chastity belt, I treat the gash with studious neglect, all the way to Nome. There, prior to the tape's painful removal, Anna flashes a genuinely startling photo—my face weather-worn, my body displaying muscles not seen since the prior year's race, and my untapped pelvic parts covered up by a small feeding dish. Now comes the sad part. If I had known about the next day's most unusual underwear contest (or was it swimming suit?) and postponed the removal, I would likely have won—paws down.

The Naked Truth

Back to 1979. My team and I get by the Muldoon wilds and proceed across the Moose Run golf course, after which we're in full view of vehicles on the Glenn Highway. Several cars are parked on the highway's shoulder, watching us, as a team is ascending a hill. We quickly catch the team and pass it, distinguishing it as a very slow one. We hear its driver exhorting his dogs to greater effort, that driver being one Gene Leonard. Gene's colorful language lends credence to the saying that in Alaska the most common name for a lead dog is "Son of a bitch." (Lending more credence is the consideration that approximately half of the lead dogs actually *are* sons of bitches.) As we pass his team we hear, "Bud, Miller, Jim Beam, Old Crow, Scotch and Soda, Gin and Tonic!" Later I will learn that Gene, formerly both a heavyweight boxer and a bar owner in the Bronx, calls his dogs "Booze Hounds." He will say that right there, on that hill, he knew he was "in the major leagues with a minor league team." More about Gene as it takes place.

In a more or less mundane fashion (if running the Iditarod is ever mundane—not!), I mush on to the checkpoint in Eagle River, 20 trail miles from Fourth Avenue in Anchorage. From the time of our arrival in the parking lot of the local VFW, we (my crew of friends and family, the dogs and I) have four hours, to the second, to get our collective butts up to Settlers' Bay, near Wasilla, for the restart. Consequently, after the dogs wolf down some food

Ascending the Hill, About to Pass Gene

(and me the same, thanks to the volunteers in the VFW dining hall) we load the team into my truck and head for Settlers' Bay.

It's less than an hour's drive, but even that can be problem-prone, as when frantically off schedule. One year, an Alaska Highway Patrolman will delay me, though he bids me on my merry way when he hears that I'm an Iditarod musher. Another time, low on fuel, I absentmindedly pump several gallons of regular gasoline into the tank of my diesel engine truck.

In the ground-breaking Iditarod of 1973, the teams sure enough travelled that part on the ground, or on the snow-covered ground, from Eagle River to the Wasilla area. It involved bridge crossing of tide-flooded rivers on the Glenn Highway, necessitating highway patrol-assisted stoppage of traffic. That plus possibly other considerations soon prompted the trucking of teams beyond Eagle River and well past the bridges, a practice that would be continued indefinitely. Another change, instituted after my '84 race, is restarting the next day, on Sunday, twenty-four hours after the Saturday "ceremonial" start in Anchorage. Yet another, the "ceremonial" will terminate in Anchorage at only eleven miles from downtown Fourth Avenue, in place of Eagle River at twenty. All of that will allow for a more leisurely first day, a less hectic takeoff for the mushers, and not one but *two* days of partying for race fans to celebrate. It also will allow me, in about 2006, to throw a monkey wrench into my restart, in Willow. Having "organized" my lines the prior evening and with only minutes to go, it is pointed out that I have places for only fourteen dogs, not the sixteen by then in harness. At the last moment, I attach the last two directly to and in front of the sled, and I take off with four dogs packed in like sardines at the back of my team. Nobody seems to notice, and we run several hours in that very unorthodox manner.

In 1979, with only four hours until the restart, there is likewise no time to retrieve equipment. So, as when lacking a regular slot for the two dogs, I simply do without what I ain't got. After driving my truck to Settler's Bay, I unload dogs and gear, hurriedly pack my sled and harness the dogs, just in time to again pull the hook and head for Nome.

Chapter Fifteen
WITH RON

Shortly after leaving the restarting line we—the dogs and I—speed downhill until leveling off on the shoreline of Knik Arm, an elongated recess of the North Pacific Ocean. At times out of control on the downhill, I thrill to the first few miles when the team is jazzed up and moving fast, around twenty miles per hour. After about an hour we are on Knik Lake and pulling in to the Knik checkpoint, by that time moving slower, around twelve or thirteen. Subsequently we will attain "cruising speed," wishfully around ten mph, but realistically eight or even less.

At Knik I sign in, required of each musher at each checkpoint to document his/her presence at said checkpoint. Also present and accounted for is Ron, and next thing you know, we both leave Knik and are zipping along the Iditarod trail. Amidst forest and on lakes and swamps, Ron and I are together, one team in front, the other not far behind. We have pretty much planned it that way, and that's how it will turn out for much of the race, for better or for worse—better for friendship and mutual support (Mushers can accept help from each other, not from anyone else.) but worse for racing, because on any given part of the trail you move at the pace of the slowest team. The point is moot, since racing has never been Ron's perception of the Iditarod. To him, the Iditarod Sled Dog Race is less race and more a grand tour of Alaska's outback. Ron may have picked up on George Attla, the sprint mushing "Spirit of the Wind" legend who ran the Iditarod twice—in 1973 and 1974—and referred to it, disparagingly, as a "big camping trip." Could it be George was just upset that he didn't win? In any event, camping will go out of style as the entire production becomes much more "racy," to the point of disqualifying "competitors" who are deemed to be "non-competing."

So, having departed Knik, Ron and I are not worrying much about making any fast tracks. In the vicinity of the Burma Road, the last road for the next 300 miles, we get confused in the dark and suspect we've traveled in a circle. Unsure if we are still on the trail to Nome and figuring we can navigate better in daylight, we stop, feed our dogs, spread our sleeping bags in our sleds, and get in. Only three or four hours into our "race," and we're camped for the night! (Another short chapter, this? Well, *only three or four hours.*)

Chapter Sixteen
DREAMS

I dream about the times, some trying, shared with my children along this same part of the trail. A teenage Margaret and friend, mushing a small team, are with me when they take a wrong turn, get lost and camp, like me in the race. After several hours I locate them, roust them from their slumber, and urge them to follow more closely, and carefully. Later we get stranded on a large lake in a gusty wind that blows a contact lens right off my eyeball. Already visually challenged by blowing snow, I'm down to only one eye. Monocular navigation makes finding our way on the dark, windswept lake difficult, but my biggest concern is management of two freaked-out teenagers. Thirty miles later, on the Yentna River and only a few miles short of our goal, my wilderness cabin on Indian Creek, we get into overflow (water above the ice) up to our knees. At minus 20°F, everything from knee down freezes solid in just minutes. By the time we reach the goal, closer to dawn than to dusk, both girls are walking like zombies. In point of fact, they are in all respects like zombies. I light a fire, but it takes hours for a small wood stove to heat up a -20° cabin. With some help from me, the girls remove their slowly thawing boots and leggings. Their bodies, also thawing and more tired than hungry, need warmth and sleep more than food. Joana, Margaret's friend, ascends to the sleeping loft. She is not seen again that night. Margaret the same, but not before sitting in front of the stove, leaning near to it while stoking the fire and warming her fingers. My weary mind's improbable but persistent premonition, from just before I go back outside to the dogs, is her nodding off and falling into the flames....

Each of my three other children will have his or her own misadventures, with and/or because of their mad dad. Son Willy undergoes his share of them. More than that, Willy and his dad share his entire, most wonderful childhood, packed with one adventure after another, both the tangible and the abstract. Willy, as well as Margaret (who will always insist she did it to please me) complete the Junior Iditarod Race, also other mushing outings, hunting sorties, and the like. While deer hunting on Kodiak Island and anticipating the end of a cold, drizzly, long-suffered day, a thirteen-year-old Willy and I are descending a cliff with heavy packs when he confides that he figures we go through the suffering *because* of the suffering, in part.

Daughter Kim, a family Worthington and I will be nearing my cabin late at night on a narrow Indian Creek. We hear hoof beats, and around creek's bend, immediately ahead, a huge bull moose bursts onto the scene. Running full-tilt and grunting rhythmically, it bears down on us, refusing to yield the trail we simultaneously occupy. This comes about so fast that I don't even think about fetching my gun, deep in my sled, as is so often the case with intimate encounters with wild animals. Two of the Worthington boys leap off their snowmachine into the deep snow beside the trail. I just hunker down with Kim, and the moose passes, only inches from us. How it gets cleanly by, without injuring any of the dogs, or us, go figure. The whole episode is over in a heartbeat, as it seems, and we continue on up the creek. This time it is -30°, and Kim's fingers and toes have ceased to function. Knowing how cold that cabin will be, she is about to lie down and give up, but God is good, as some friends arrived a few hours earlier. The cabin's interior is warm, and so is a spaghetti supper! Mushing junkets don't always end so happily for Kim, as we shall see.

Other youngsters will be the arguably benign beneficiaries of the Lanier mushing school, and often in that same Knik-Yentna region. One Gunnar Johnson, a family friend since his diaper days, will live with me, my family and my dogs for a whole year while he's figuring out what to do with his life. That March of 1991, when he runs the Iditarod using mostly my dogs, Gunnar realizes it is not going to be professional mushing. He will not stop dabbling in dogs, though, and he goes out on the trails with me, his friend Dave Hruska and my son, Jimmy, each winter for a week, to remind him that's enough. A spin-off is his writing career, with several published magazine articles, two of which stem from our mostly good times together (Uma and Me, *Mushing*, Nov/Dec, 2006 and Mushing Injuries, a Case Study, *Mushing*, May, 2007). Gunnar will also serve as my crewman for more than one commercial fishing season. He will sum up his take on the whole thing by stating, "I found out I had signed on with Captain Ahab." Another spin-off is Dave's dubbing my cabin, admittedly elemental, a "wooden tent."

During Gunnar's enlightening stay with us he will appear at my door after a training run from hell, accompanied by Kim. With a face both anguished and apologetic, he allows as how I now have one less dog. Much earlier that day he and Kim trucked to Knik, harnessed a team, and shot off down that same part of the Iditarod trail. After several miles at well below zero they stopped, set the hook, and poured some hot beverage from a thermos. Things were going well, and they were enjoying life. Too well, and too much enjoyment. They neglected a cardinal rule: Never stand to the rear of the sled! With Kim and Gunnar thusly misplaced and cups in hand, the dogs yanked that hook loose and took off. The sight of the disappearing dog team was disheartening and also disastrous, in the end. With Gunnar carrying the thermos and Kim's cup in her perpetually freezing fingers, her warm mitts bouncing ahead in the sled, they gave chase. They ran, then trudged through the snow for a long time. With guidance from some people who had seen the runaway team, they finally found it. Praying that all was well, they discovered otherwise. One of the dogs had become tangled in its harness and was beyond any possibility of resuscitation. In the event of such entanglement with the musher on the sled, you simply stop and untangle the dog. But with no one in the sled, there was no stopping, and no untangling. The tragic, unusual occurrence made Kim feel as though her house pet had run out into the street and been run over by a passing vehicle.

On the return to the truck, Kim sat in the sled and cradled the dead dog, stiff and stark, in her lap. Like I said, mushing does not always end happily for Kim. Getting home would be the end of a bad, sad day, also the end of Kim's mushing career. She's happy to travel other trails, but I doubt she will ever again be on a dogsled.

I'll have other protégés. One Gajus Worthington, son of a former commercial fishing and hunting partner, will run the Jr. Iditarod race with my dogs and under my tutelage. And in the next millennium, along will come our foreign exchange student from Spain, Guillermo Anton Fernandez. Living an entire school year *en nuestra casa*, Guillermo becomes both a family member and a dog musher. In addition to the Jr. Iditarod he runs two other races, one of them an adult, 300-miler. Guillermo, Jimmy and I will share lots of good times on the mushing trail. Again, mostly good.

Chapter Seventeen
STOVES

After several hours' dreamy sleep, I begin to wake up. Several hours! In all my subsequent Iditarods, unheard of. Most sleep will be nap-like. One hour, two at most. In this, my first Iditarod, aka my "Last Great Camping Trip," the waking process is nonetheless the same as in subsequent races, as much a dream as the dreams. Total disorientation, with no idea of where, what, how, even who, and definitely not why. Reality takes hold, gradually. I'm in a dogsled on the Iditarod Trail, running the Iditarod Race, motored by mutts and I'm Jim Lanier, wannabe long distance musher. Then, "Ron, you awake?"... "H'm?"... "We'd better get going."..."Yeah." And so we do. Out of our sleds, we shove our gear back into them, hook up the dogs, and move out—we hope toward Nome.

Our spirits buoyed by a lovely, sunny day, Ron and I head for Flathorn Lake. Along the way, we gawk at the up-close and awe-inspiring sight of Sleeping Lady, a mountain of reclining feminine shape, prominent on the Anchorage skyline. Out of the forest, across Flathorn and a large swamp, then down a precipitous bank onto the Susitna River, it's mid-morning. On the river's far side are a few people bedecked by smoke, as from a wood fire. (Many years in the future, I will disremember whether it was an official checkpoint. If so, it would have been called Susitna Station.) When we pull up to those folks, they react like it *is* a checkpoint. "Bib number? How many dogs? Took you guys a while to get here. Everything all right?" It's a pleasant day, we know we're on the right trail, and we're moving, so "We're all right." But I notice they seem worried about us. I'm wondering if *we* should be worried. Something else I notice is that there are *two* fires, one wood, the other a sled. That's right, a sled—on fire, or more true to fact, smoldering. One of the mushers (Bud Smyth?) tried to get a leg up on the competition with a stove that would cook his dogs' next meal on the run, in the sled, while moving down the trail. As one might have foreseen, his entire conveyance caught fire and burned to the runners. He was forced to abandon sled and withdraw from the race.

All Eyes on the Sleeping Lady

Ron and I head up the Yentna River. Before long, we call a halt, by the riverbank and in the neighborhood of the soon-to-be homesteaded Yentna Station. We pull dog food out of our sleds and feed our animals. Years later my equipment—sleds, lines, harnesses, food, heat source (for boiling water to thaw the frozen food), the dogs too—will become markedly improved, even hi-tech. In 1979, my sled is made from Alaska birch, by Jerry Riley. It is very flexible, a good thing, but some of its parts are prone to breakage by the trauma of the trail. My heat source varies from a wood fire to a Coleman stove. Coaxing a Coleman to start at 20 below or colder is an art. It can be very frustrating. The minute the burners are lit, I fill two several-gallon Hill's Brothers coffee tins, one side cut away, with snow and set them on the stove. Bulky and poorly balanced above the stove, they become even more precarious when I remove them, one now full of boiling water, add meat and /or fish, and wobble from dog to dog in deep, soft snow, ladling a meal to each one. Often, too often, my boots get ladled as well. Then I examine all the animals, see to their needs, check my gear, eat some food myself, and try to catch a few winks. Soon it's time to go, and we're back on the trail, gliding soundlessly up the ice-bound Yentna and watching the sunset. Taking darkness as a cue for another break, we take one and again sleep through the night.

Hill's Brothers on the Coleman on the Yentna

Chapter Eighteen
A FOWL EXPERIENCE

Lanier's made a million memories and relates many a tale,
Like the time a flock of chickens lured his team off the trail.
A dozen dogs stuck in a coop in a scene that was most whacky.
A few hens wound up fricasseed, and Jim lost two hours to Mackey.
—by Hurricane Dave, as in The Cheechako Chronicles

Now close to the mouth of Lake Creek (I would know that only years later, this being my original foray into the Yentna River region.), I have no appreciation for all the fine miseries I will put up with here in the years ahead. One of the finest will occur when I veer off the river trail, mush up the riverbank, and stop in front of a cabin. It is part of Riversong Lodge, then owned and operated by Carl and Kirsten Dixon, later of Wintersong Lodge (Finger Lake checkpoint) fame, as mentioned in chapter twelve. Sensing that someone is inside, I knock on the door, which is opened by Riversong's winter caretaker. Such caretakers are often short on company and welcome a stranger (not all, some being in that situation for a reason). At any rate, this guy invites me to come in for coffee and to sit for a spell, and I don't mind if I do.

Finished with both the coffee and the sitting, and back outside at my sled, I hear the caretaker counsel, "No need to turn your team around. Just go forward. That trail you're on makes a right turn, just after the main lodge building, and then takes you back down onto the river." "Thanks," says I. "I'll take your advice." I pull the snow hook, releasing the sled, and sure 'nuff, we turn to the right and head for the river. We are also headed, fatefully, for several large barnyard geese, strutting smack dab in the middle of the trail. The dogs go bananas and charge. With a relatively soft trail surface, there's no way on God's green earth I can hold them back. Then the geese, honking loudly and as if following a script, waddle off the trail to a nearby chicken coop, with chickens. I urge the leaders, "On by!" which means, "Go straight ahead, and don't even think about going after those birds!" The leaders gamely obey my command, but the team dogs cry fowl and pull off for the poultry. With a "What the hell!" the leaders abandon all and join the chase. Totally out of my control, out of any control whatsoever, they chase the chickens through their small rectangular door and into the coop. Before I can snap out of my stupefied amazement, the leaders are followed in rapid succession by the next several members of the team.

So I find myself butt-down on the snow, feet propped up on both sides of the little door, yanking on the gangline and extracting the team from the chicken coop—one dog at a time and each with a squawking, bleeding chicken in its mouth. Noticing the caretaker, I start to apologize for the ruckus and the chickens, but he preempts me with, "It's okay. This is the most fun I've had all winter."

Chapter Nineteen
SKWENTNA

At midday on Monday, day three of the '79 Iditarod, we arrive at the Skwentna checkpoint. A full two days and two nights—forty-eight hours—and we are less than one hundred miles into our journey. Years later, in the next millennium, I will reach Skwentna in as little as *six* hours, albeit the "modern-day" run there will be somewhat shorter. Even so, forty-eight hours! No wonder the race officials are still worried.

Only a handful of other mushers are at the checkpoint, most teams having moved on some time ago. Ron and I care for our dogs and then walk up the high, steep riverbank. As we do so, I am most impressed when I note the departure of a musher (after his twenty-four-hour rest, the twenty-four hours mandated for each team by race rules). I believe it's Ken Chase, a veteran musher from Anvik, on the Yukon River. For some reason, Ken parked his team up on the high bank. He releases his team and rides his sled down that bank, onto the river and out of sight on the trail to somewhere. He makes it look easy, and I ask myself, "If that's easy, in effect *routine* for him, what's going to be difficult?" It forebodes tougher times to come.

Atop the riverbank is a log building, the residence of Joe Delia, trapper and Lord High Just About Everything Else of Skwentna, a way-off-the-road, woodsy, riverside community of about a hundred odd souls. Joe is the Skwentna checker, the person who checks all the teams into each checkpoint and otherwise keeps track of things. He is also the guy who opens his home to the race, year after year. Already a legend in 1979 (very much so to Ron), Joe Delia will become a member of the Iditarod Hall of Fame.

Inside, besides Joe himself, is an abundance of delicious and most welcome food and drink, served by a bevy of beauties, all of whom are most hospitable. Following the feast and its attendant banter, as good as the food, we find the sofa and nod off. By the time we awaken and partake of more repast, checkpoint procrastination is at an end. Even Ron admits it's time to head back down to the river where our dogs are snoozing soundly on the straw we laid down for them, the straw provided at each checkpoint by the ITC, the Iditarod Trail Committee.

Skwentna is the site of a future photo op. My son Willy, at about age ten, will be there with me, and as we talk to Joe Redington, Sr., founder and Father of the Iditarod, I take a snapshot of Joe and Willy. It develops into a fine photograph, but I will lose track. I'd like to recapture it.

Another time, Joe Garnie, the colorful competitor from the Eskimo community of Teller, will be kneeling in the snow, chopping up fish and seal meat with his ax. He deplores how he can't run the race without a screw up and states that otherwise he could do really well. And Emmitt Peters, the "Yukon River Fox" from the Athabaskan Indian village of Ruby, grumbles that he's out of snaps. (That's brass *snaps*, not *schnapps*, an even worse calamity.) The trail to Skwentna went overland through the woods, with lots of tight turns around trees. This resulted in *snapped* snaps, the ones on dogs' necklines, when they tried the wrong side. I have plenty of the little gadgets, and Emmitt expresses his gratitude for the ones I give him.

Then there's the time when Larry Smith, the taciturn Canadian "Cowboy," is even more taciturn than usual as he sits separate from all the other teams, fuming. Cowboy, and Susan Butcher too, missed a turn prior to Skwentna and went twenty-some miles out of their way. Swenson, number one into Skwentna, reports that he saw them taking that wrong turn in front of him. In a wry whisper he says, "I called out for them to turn around, that they were headin' the wrong way," and he indicates he feels just awful about it. Sure, Rick.

Again moving into darkness and up the (now Skwentna) River, we round a bend where five years later, in 1984, I will be subjected to my first sexual activity, while racing sled dogs. That's the year I drive Norman Vaughan's team. At the prerace musher's meeting, I had asked Swenson for some advice. Norman's leader, Kansas, was in season, and I asked Rick what to do. He said, "Leave her in your kennel. But she's your best leader, right?" "Uh huh," I mumbled. "Then run her in wheel (the back of the team) for the first few days." The idea is that if an attractive female is in the rear, the males will not *smell* her rear when moving down the trail. They will disregard her completely, and it works well with Kansas in that position, until after leaving Skwentna. Rounding that river bend, I briefly take my eyes off the team, and then it happens. All the dogs, led by my two male leaders, lust suddenly to the rear and to Kansas. Within seconds, all sixteen dogs are in one big breeding, biting ball—the gangline, tugs and necklines hopelessly intertwined. Now, this situation is not so unusual, nor hopeless, but this time is different. I'm out on the middle of a river with no tree or bush to which I can anchor the sled. Furthermore, the weather has been very warm, 40° F, so the deep snow covering the river ice is mush and will not hold a hook, no matter how deeply driven. I try to undo the mess, but as I begin to unravel a few critters, another mating and three fights break out, the hook releases, and I'm back to square one. For literally hours I'm stuck there with my messed-up team, straining to keep the sex-crazed, snarling animals from killing each other, or me. Other mushers come along, but they can't help without risking the same fate. This whole episode began around 9 PM, and it's not until midnight that I am able to secure the sled and make some measure of order out of chaos. Then, with my procreating pooch in lead, we run like the wind, all the males doing their damnedest to catch her. All *I* have to do is stay glued to the sled and pray Kansas doesn't turn around, a paramount concern with that arrangement. It is 45 miles to Finger Lake, the next checkpoint. She doesn't turn, and we get there *fast*. After that, I figure the best way to maintain order will be to allow Kansas free rein at the procreating, and I let her lie next to my male leader, Oley.

Leaders in Love

Chapter Twenty
A BONFIRE

Skwentna to Finger features some river and one small lake but is mostly swamps, with intervening forested portages. In the portages the bell rings on the opening round of what I call dipsy doodles, where the trail suddenly goes downhill, and simultaneously left or right. This demands some adroit sled handling, in order to avoid hitting a tree or tipping over and losing the team. It's a taste of things to come. Another taste is that of my medicines. Stocked in my sled's pharmacy are Naprosyn, an Advil-type drug for a back condition I've had since my twenties, and Ovaban, a female hormone to prevent your girls from going into heat. A few things about this.

First, the Naprosyn helps me, and I've taken it for years. Second, the Ovaban must help too, since in 1979 I have no amorous bitches in the team. Third, both the Naprosyn and the Ovaban come in the form of small yellow pills. After a few days the dogs are feeling no pain, and I'm a tenor! At least I haven't gone into heat. All kidding aside, the gait of one of my dogs looks labored. Examination yields a diagnosis of a pulled muscle, or something. At this point in time, unlike in Iditarods yet to be, it is perfectly legit to administer a nonsteroidal analgesic, like Naprosyn, to your teammates, or to yourself for that matter. So I do administer, and in thirty minutes I have a seemingly healthy, happy, normal-gaited and hardworking dog. I sympathize with why such drugs will be banned, but does it ever help!

Around halfway to Finger Lake is an open place where a number of locals from Shell Lake stoke an enormous bonfire, drink beer and wait for the race to reach them. As Anna preps for her second Iditarod in 2004, I will tell her the bonfire might afford a warm, friendly refuge for some timeout. What I don't tell her is that those locals traditionally pass the beaver hat to collect money, a prize for the first arrival. Without any expectation of reward, Anna moves fast and gets to that bonfire before anyone else. Spotting the flames, which cannot be missed, and hearing all the whooping and hollering, she keeps moving, to flee down the trail to some safe and sane, quiet, peaceful haven posthaste. But as she flees, several revelers whoop right at her, asking her to stop. One of them leaps on a snowmachine and gives chase, then hollers out and "dogs" her team as she proceeds past the fire. More angry than frightened by all this, Anna hollers back, doubtless employing a few four letter Russian words, and she announces that she would stop *over his dead body*. Just before Anna and team exit the opening, the snowmachiner flings an envelope into her sled, claiming it's her prize money. Not believing it for an instant, Anna doesn't give the envelope another thought. Days later, when at Nikolai (and close to the front of the race), she spies that envelope, crumpled up in the grungy bottom of her sled bag. Amazed to discover that it *does* contain money, about $500, her amazement turns to remorse. After the race Anna takes pains to contact her Shell Lake supporters, to apologize and to thank them for her winnings, and for their persistence.

Sunrise, Somewhere East of Finger

Chapter Twenty-One
FINALLY FINGER

Finger is a fine-looking little lake, a mile or so in diameter, and it is surrounded by snow-clad hills, foothills of the Alaska Range just ahead. We park our dogs on the snowed-over ice below the checkpoint cabin. It is the domicile of Gene Leonard, the boozehound musher and former prizefighter/bar owner, also of his mail-order bride, June. When Gene moved to Alaska years ago he got lonely, so he placed a "Wife Wanted" ad in an Anchorage newspaper. Several auditions later, he made his selection and was happy ever after. Gene and June operate the Finger Lake weather reporting station, and they have benefitted from life in the wilderness, or so it would appear. That station will be the scene of an Iditarod Trail wedding when race entrant Jan Masek stops long enough (Is his twenty-four-hour stop long enough?) to marry another racer, Anvik musher Beverly Jerue Masek, the state legislator. Norman Vaughan performs the ceremony.

The Leonards will eventually move south to a warmer clime, in Tennessee, like Sam McGee to his Plumtree (*The Cremation of Sam McGee;* Robert Service). Their weather station will then come into the ownership of the Dixons and be named Wintersong Lodge. In year 2000, with Anna in her first race, I bum a flight to Finger, in the aeronautical arms of Iditarod Air Force pilot, Bill Mayer. I'm accompanied by my three-year-old son, Jimmy, and Anna's mother, Galena, on a visit from Russia. We fly to Finger and then wait several hours for an overdue Anna. Having taken a false trail (like Cowboy and Susan) and crashing once or twice, she is upset and uptight, but upbeat and game for more. Though happy (and astounded) to see us, she is focused mainly on her race. After caring for her dogs, a snack and an attempt at a nap, she leaves Finger as she arrived—in the dark, and in more ways than one. She seems drained and moderately disoriented, and I must admit to being worried about her. Her mother the same, wondering anew why in the world her daughter would want to do a thing so crazy as run the Iditarod.

Then, with Anna back on the trail, Galena gets around to the raison d'etre, besides Anna, for our being at Wintersong Lodge. Kirsten Dixon, the lodge owner, is a world-renowned chef. Her culinary style is both Alaskan and very French, with Russian cuisine never, if ever, on the menu. But in the future it could be, because Galena shows Kirsten how to prepare borscht, a Russian soup, and other yummy stuff like piroshky, sort of a Russian ravioli. They surmount the language barrier by the showing, versus the telling, of how to do, and they both enjoy the experience. Jimmy and I enjoy the borscht, and the piroshky. I will once send out enough of those little piroshkies to eat one every five miles, from Anchorage to Nome.

In 1979 we hang out for a while at the Finger Lake checkpoint, a considerable while, as is becoming routine with Ron. Gene Leonard pulls in, and comes home, with his boozehounds. This means he will need to convince those hounds that they should get up and leave their oh-so-familiar, oh-so-comfortable doggie dens when it's time to go. Leave they do, however, and me too, but not before making an unsettling discovery. Up to now, in my short mushing career, I have not acquired any familiarity with booties. My dogs have never worn booties, and I look askance at them, as a crutch for canines either undertrained or genetically underendowed, like perhaps a poodle. It comes as a rude awakening, one of many, when I remark that several of my animals have sore feet. It starts as a thing called a "split." In dog mushing parlance, a split is a longitudinal erosion deep in the recess of a paw, over a tendon. If untended, a split can lead to an infected distress that obliges an otherwise willing dog to be unable to contribute, and to then become a passenger in your sled. In years to come everyone will use booties on all their dogs prophylactically, at race start and thereafter, to prevent splits from ever developing. At Finger in 1979, however, I am suddenly and unexpectedly appreciative of why I took those "crutches" with me, and I start using them. Booties will come to be made with Velcro closures, but in '79 I fasten them with adhesive tape. The taped bootie is secure but onerous to apply and remove. I'm taping and untaping at each stop, and by mid-race on half of the feet in my team at well below zero. It becomes another finger-freezing, mind-numbing task.

A Passenger in the Sled

Chapter Twenty-Two
MOOSE MADNESS

You move quietly down the moonlit trail, with only the soft swish of the runners and the padded "pat, pat, pat" of paws on snow. It is surreal, out of this world, a universe removed from life's earthly experience. Things are going well, for now, and you are all but complacent, your guard down. Deep in your sled is a loaded handgun, minimum .357 magnum caliber, but that too is far from your conscious concern, not to mention your reach. The quiet is complete, too complete. When reality checks in, sparked by a shadowy form alongside a tree, you harken to why you brought the pistol. Moose. Big, dark, hulking Alaska moose. Along the Iditarod are many wild animals—moose and caribou, wolves and wolverines, bison and bears, and others. Some species are seldom seen due to their secretive, shy temperaments and behavior. Wolves avoid human contact, and bears hibernate in winter, thank God. But moose, now that's a different story. They are encountered frequently, often at close range. When it's a cow protecting a calf, it can portend a very bad outcome. The mother moose views your dogs as a pack of wolves, and she will often charge, right into your team. Mama usually passes through quickly, but not every time. She may stop and stomp, her sharp hooves meting death and destruction, breaking bodies, bones and brains in just seconds. At this juncture, you must take action. There are stories of mushers wielding tree limbs, axes and anything else at hand, but the definitive tool is your loaded gun.

It's along the Skwentna to Finger to Rainy Pass portion of Iditarod where the most moose run-ins materialize, due to lots of moose, narrow wooded trail and heavy snowfall, resulting in the animals' reluctance to leave the traveled thoroughfare for strenuous plowing through the deep snow. It is in this general region where Susan Butcher will suffer her calamitous moose meeting in 1985. That moose gets into the middle of her team and refuses to leave. By the time another musher arrives, with a weapon to dispatch the moose, several of Susan's dogs are injured, and one is dead. Susan scratches at the next checkpoint, her high hopes for victory that year scratched as well, and destiny dictating that Libby Riddles will go on to become the first woman to call herself an Iditarod champion.

No musher wants to confront a moose, much less kill one. This is partly because you are then obligated by Iditarod rules, also by Alaska State law, to gut the animal so the meat can be salvaged, and for someone more deserving than you. The same year of Susan's debacle, and only a few days later, I will have my moose meeting most catastrophic, for the moose. Not in the race that year, my team and I will be near the road from Willow, Alaska, to Hatcher Pass. That year's excessively deep snow undoubtedly accounts for what happens, as well as what happened to Susan. As I level off on a hilltop, I see a moose on the trail ahead, and I hit the brake. The moose runs away, and I follow, hoping the animal will exit the trail. It doesn't and soon is in front of me again. When it disappears over the next rise, I follow once more. This is repeated three or four times until the moose has had enough and comes straight at me. I flip the sled on its side and plop down on it, to stop my surging team from charging. Having dug my .357 mag from out of the sled, I fire a warning shot over the moose's head. The shot does not dissuade, and when the moose steps into my team, I shoot to kill. Blood spurts with each bullet, and the animal staggers but keeps coming, all the way through the snarling, snapping dogs. Just before the moose staggers into me, I aim point-blank and place the last bullet between its eyes. It swoons and falls, dying, on my sled. I must say, that qualifies as a fairly exciting episode.

With the moose thrashing its last, my dogs all come close, crouching in a semicircle. A few of the more inquisitive and daring dogs venture close enough to wrest a quick mouthful of moose hair. I must move the carcass off the sled, but I can't, not with adult moose averaging more than half a ton. So I set to work gutting the thing, taking care that the insides of the moose do not foul the insides of my sled bag. The guttation accomplished, I still cannot move the gutless beast until leverage obtained with a spruce bough does the trick. Then, after I get the team back into some semblance of order, we sled the short distance to the Hatcher Pass Road and to a phone, and I dial up the state troopers. After I detail the "coordinates" of the crime scene, the troopers notify the next name on their list of families in need. A few hours later I revisit that scene and talk to the people dicing up the meat. When I tell them I am their benefactor, they thank me profusely and ask how they can repay. I reply, "A couple of steaks would do very nicely." At next morning's breakfast, moose steak and eggs will never taste better.

Among numerous other moosings, the most unforgettable will take place right in Anchorage on the Tudor Track trails, in what is now Bicentennial Park. In the darkness of a midwinter Alaska evening, with sundown around 3 PM, I round a corner and run into not only a moose but two moose, a cow and a calf. I stop just as the cow lowers her head and charges, right past the team and then past me. This puts me *between* the cow and the calf, not a desirable location. Before I can react, the calf also runs abreast the team, to rejoin its mother. As it goes by, I keep one eye on mama and am more astonished than hurt when the calf thumps into my shoulder. That's my one and only time to have been hit by a moose. Well now, with both mama and her offspring to my rear and an open trail before me, I release the sled and we're off, like a dirty shirt.

Super excited by all this, the team sprints as dogs possessed. We fly down the trail, over small rises and around turns, covering more than a mile in no time. I begin to relax, but then I hear hoof beats. Turning around, I see her, an angry mama moose at roughly fifty yards and closing fast. "Hike! Get up!" I beg the dogs, and they sprint even faster, but not fast enough. I look back again. She's gaining! Thirty yards…twenty. Hooves pounding, chest heaving, nostrils snorting, eyes red coals in my headlamp's flickering light. Into my mind springs an ethereal apparition, that of the Headless Horseman and I, musher Ichabod Crane! I know that just a short distance ahead is a road crossing, if only I can get there. I do get to the road and cross it, but to my horror, so does the apparition, and now the specter is a scant ten yards from catching me. Very soon we will be on a footbridge, spanning Anchorage's Campbell Creek, if we can make it that far. I hear the moose's madness, I see the bridge, I'm on the bridge and then on its other side and…and the moose must have turned back. I don't see it or hear it, or feel it. A moose on the loose, but no longer on my tail. That has been real creature discomfort and real scary, every bit as scary as I've tried to describe it.

As to wild animals, there's another rather prickly problem, potentially more harmful than even a mad moose, as I see it. Porcupine. I've had three unhappy meetings with those quilty critters, and I'm not eager for a fourth. Daytime is not so troubling because porcies are nocturnal and not often on the dog trails in daylight. If so, I spot them in plenty of time to stop, and often they are safely up in a tree. But at night, that's another matter. They are on the prowl, or on the waddle you might say, and your only warning comes when the entire front of your team compresses into a small dark ball to the side of the trail—in a wild feeding frenzy. By then, it's too late. The porcupine is dead, and the dogs wish they were dead too.

A multitude of quills protrude from muzzles, noses, eyeballs, legs, etc. No part of a dog's anatomy is immune. Some poor pooches are so distraught that I need to restrain them and carry them home. Then comes the night's main event, in my garage with extractions, utilizing the instrument that best grabs, quill by quill. One person is the extractor, and another holds tight to the wriggling, panicked extractee. Many quills get stuck inside the mouth, a dicey proposition with all those sharp canines, so to say. The whole procedure can take many hours, ruining any designs you may have had on a decent night's sleep. What's more, you never remove all the quills because some of them get buried under skin or mucous membrane and later migrate deeper into various body structures. The end result can be a permanently disabled dog, never again a member your team. One time it's a disabled *me* when, several days after a session in my garage, my right arm becomes sore, and I dig up a quill, interred in the soreness. Over all the years, my tally of dogs retired by wild animal injuries is moose one, porcupines three. Therefore, bring on the moose!

Chapter Twenty-Three
DAMAGE CONTROL, OR LACK OF

On the trail out of Finger we come upon that opening round of the significant ups and downs. Not emotional ups and downs—they come later. I'm referring to the trail itself. You see, in dog mushing there are certain clues. One of them is when your entire team suddenly disappears. This is a clue that you too are about to disappear, over the same precipice. Your knee-jerk reaction is to spit out "Shoot" (not really) and tense up for the next second until you and the sled drop precipitously downhill. Even though at least one foot is conveying your entire body weight down onto the brake, you might drop faster than the dogs, and if this is of sufficient duration you can catch and even pass some of them. One time, again near Alaska's Hatcher Pass, I go over the edge and down a mountainside and catch up to the lead dogs as the sled and I tumble in near free-fall.

For the first hour after Finger Lake there are several of these panic zones. They culminate at "The Steps," where mushers must negotiate some switchbacks while descending the canyon wall down to Happy River. The spot is notorious for spectacular spills and smashed sleds, prompting helicopter-borne camera crews to wait in ambush for their unsuspecting subjects. In 1979 I have not even heard of it, but I see it coming when my lead dogs and I are suddenly traveling in opposite directions, another clue. I brace for the 180-degree turn, and it comes all too soon. Though thrilling, "The Steps" cause me no harm, and we level off onto the playful little Happy as it spills, frozen, into the much larger Skwentna River.

At the Mouth of the Happy River

At that flat, calm, serene, "Happy" river mouth mushers will often camp for a few hours, me included. It is also where, on several occasions, a camper will ponder what's to be done with his or her sled, ravaged by "The Steps" or prior nasty spots. Some sleds are damaged so severely that their drivers are forced to cut losses and go home. An example is my neighbor in Chugiak, Melinda Miles, in 2004. Another is Karin Hendrickson in 2010. It's not only sleds that are damaged. Mushers too, as in Doug Swingley's rib fracture, Dee Dee Jonrowe's hand fracture, and Rick Swenson's collar bone fracture.

Speaking of four-time champ Swingley, one year I'll take five at Happy and throw my dogs a snack when he comes along and passes by, muttering "How ya doin', old man?" I shoot back something equally flattering and then fall in behind him. Leaving the riverbed, the trail rises up a high bank and goes on in the same fashion, far up and out of the canyon. It is the steepest climb in the entire Iditarod, and I'm determined to keep up with Doug, at least till concluding the ascent. Urging my team to maximum effort, I'm off the sled, pumping my legs for all they're worth, pushing upward and breaking a sweat. I look up and, by golly, I'm staying with him. Makes me feel pretty good, until I look again. The son of a bitch is standing on the runners!

You may recall my being worried for Anna when, in 2000, she departs Finger Lake. I even ask another musher, who left Finger after Anna, to keep an eye out for her. Prophetic enough, a short time later, on one of those dipsy doodles, she smashes into a tree trunk and fractures a finger. Every now and then, I will be reminded it was on her *left* hand when I look at her left fourth finger, rigid and straight as an arrow. Anna will be forever thankful it was not her middle finger. Her mishap becomes prophesy fulfilled when the guy whom I asked to keep an eye out for her comes along and helps pry her sled off the wrong side of the tree.

One way or another, Ron and I manage our way to Rainy Pass checkpoint, on Puntilla Lake. I say "one way or another" because my recollection of our getting from Finger to Rainy is fuzzy—maybe uneventful, maybe terrible. The most trying parts of Iditarod are often like that, like childbirth? Such a denying defense mechanism can help a person return for more, next season. Another aspect of the race, sometimes better forgotten, are the hallucinations and hallucination-like dreams. Such are common and reported by almost everyone who has ever made it to Nome. You hear, see and just plain imagine all sorts of things. From that '79 race, one such thing stands out, from the fuzziness. The trail to Puntilla is on a map of Rhode Island, and we are mushing from one corner of that small state to another. Sounds crazy, and I know it's not reality, but I can't mush past it. Not only hallucinatory, it is also delusional. Resolved by Rainy Pass, this particular dream-like "*hallusion*" does not recur. But I'm not out of the weird woods, not by any means.

After the Happy River crossing and initiated by the "Swingley Ascent," the trail is a continuation of the ups and downs prior to Happy. It will vary, from year to year, in its degree of difficulty, but it has what it takes to be right up there. One year, around 2005, it will be a ten. About halfway to Rainy the trail turns downhill and to the right, with a few tree branches hidden under the snow on the inside aspect of the turn. If you touch the brake (which I do) instead of letting your sled track forward (which I don't), the front of the sled can lodge into the right (wrong) side of the branches (which is what happens). The entire team just hangs there, below me, pulling downward with all its might as the sled is jammed deeper into that wrong side. I can't pull the sled free, so with ax in hand I position myself for a few whacks. To get leverage, this position must be in front of and below the sled, which means that once released, the sled will blastoff down the hill—without me. I see no alternative, so I let both of my two snow hooks dangle free on their ropes, outside of the sled, and proceeded to whack away. After about whack number nine, I am left alone after my whole outfit shoots down that hill, as if from a gun. At the bottom, the dogs turn to the left, because that's where the trail goes, and the sled rolls over into a tree.

At the same instant, the team jerks it sideways. This is the moment of truth because if the hooks fail to seize the snow, I will not regain the sled as the dogs pull it away, to Rainy Pass checkpoint I fear, a good ten miles distant. But God is still good. One of the hooks catches something and holds. Gazelle-like, I leap down the hill, quickly scan the sled for damage (incredibly, none), pull the holding hook, and we're on the road again.

I'm not always so lucky. A few years later I take a tumble on that same hill, and I *do* lose the team. A certain type of conditioned response follows. You spring to your feet and yell, "Whoa! Whoa!" knowing full well the futility of it all. Sled dogs do respond to the "Whoa" command, but only if the brake is applied simultaneously. When suddenly free of your limited control, however, there's no way in hell's half acre they are going to stop. Nevertheless, and still into futility, you keep on "whoaing" while you take off, running. Running, in all your insulating clothes. This is no good, and you begin to overheat. You stop both the whoaing and the running, and watch your only means of transportation vanish around the next bend. Then it's a matter of resigned plodding as you remove one piece of clothing after another, hoping against hope that the dogs will somehow stop so you will not need to plod for hours. This time I plod only thirty minutes when hope springs eternal and I see it, my entire team tied out neatly between two trees. John Baker had passed me, and when my riderless team caught up to him he latched on to it, made fast his team, and tied mine to the trees. Thanks, Johnny!

A Lake Nestled in Alaska Range Foothills, a Respite from The Steps and Other Nasties

Chapter Twenty-Four
THINGS GO BUMP IN THE DARK

The Rainy checkpoint is situated on the shore of Puntilla Lake, which affords a choice landing strip for the single engine aircraft, on skis, of the Iditarod Air Force. The pilots are volunteers who ferry supplies, race personnel and dropped dogs up and down the trail. Same as the mushers, they come from all walks of life and each year join together to experience the trail from the air; and like the mushers, the vets, the race judges, checkers and other assorted Iditarod junkies, the pilots have their own unique perspective on the event. I know several of them, but I must admit that only infrequently have I had, or taken time during the race to engage in much meaningful dialogue. Those flyboys, with an occasional flygirl, must have tall tales to tell, and I should like to hear them.

Our dogs are curled up on their beds of straw, near the lakeshore. For mushers there is a small cabin in which we can break out our bedding. Floor space is at a premium, with almost more people feet than square feet. It is debatably preferable to our sleds, with a marginal stove and a door that drafts in the cold as each musher enters or exits. I shouldn't complain, though, because even after three nights of inexcusably long, though sometimes fitful and dreamful sleep, we humans—Ron and I—are spacing out and can snooze soundly; and by this point, in all my future races, the snoozing will have eluded me completely. Maybe Ron has the right approach.

We leave Rainy Pass checkpoint and commence the climb, some twenty miles long and in places steep, up into Rainy Pass proper. The weather, as from the race start, is fair and calm with moderate temperatures, above zero F. during the day and down to minus twenty at night. We've said good-by to the forest and the protection of its trees, and now hello to the above timber-line exposure of a wide open mountain vista, with vision in all corners of the compass limited only by the awe-inspiring peaks of the Alaska Range. This is where early racers were met by a chill factor of -130 degrees, where Norman

Vaughan was rescued after being lost for days up the wrong valley, and where Jim and Anna will live through their *one snowmachine* fiasco.

In general, the future trail will become better marked, compared to the race's early years. However, the marking can create its own glitches. There will come a time when, keeping an eye on the markers, I am reassured that I'm doing well until I see a team coming right at me, yet another clue. This one suggests that one of us is going the wrong way. Worse than that, *both* of us are going the wrong way, made clear to me when J. Baker meets me head-on and laments, "Jim, we made a wrong turn." Retracing our tracks, we reproach ourselves considerably. The marking at the juncture of the trails to Ptarmigan Pass (Hell's Gate) and Rainy was misleading, unfortunate for us and several others.

Ron and I avoid any false moves and enter the valley that leads to the pass of choice. As mentioned, winds are calm, but evidence abounds that such is not always the case. Recent gales have sculptured the driven snow into sastrugi, the solid, sharp-edged ridges into which our sleds smash, ridge after ridge and mile after mile. Otherwise, things are proceeding satisfactorily when my leaders balk and step off into deep snow. I join them and nearly stumble into the open creek the dogs are refusing to enter. Smart dogs. I might as well have stumbled in because there's nothing for it but to walk those leaders into the creek and pull 'em through. Two by two, the entire team runs the watery gauntlet, each dog getting just as wet as its musher. Being dogs, they just shake it off, literally. For me it's not that easy, so when I spy a team stopped up ahead, I join it.

I throw the dogs a snack, a snack recommended by the great woodsman, Wolverine Riley. Sticks of butter, one to each dog. Jerry told me that dogs love butter and that it provides a substantial amount of calories. Well, duh…. He also suggested that I save the last of it for myself. So, that last icy-hard stick firmly in my grip, I gnaw away and succeed in gagging down most of it. In a few minutes it hits me, a disgusting aftertaste that stays with me for hours, the memory for years. It doesn't seem to faze the dogs, but I will not eat butter for some time.

Then, after tending to my wet feet and at this point separate from Ron, I strike up a conversation with the other musher. I learn that the guy is a trapper type who lives a 24/7 bush life, running his trapline with his dog team. As he hurriedly readies to depart, he insinuates that I have embarrassed him, that he should in no way be at the back of the pack with a city-slickin' cheechako like me. I will forget his name, if I ever knew it, and will not run into him later in the race, nor in other Iditarods. It could be he withdrew, humiliated, and never raced again. Such chance meetings can have lasting consequences. Maybe I terminated his entire mushing career.

I get moving, and now the ascension begins in earnest. The final thirty to forty minutes to the top are the steepest. As with most climbs, there are several false summits, where just over the next rise must surely be the top, but isn't. In sled dog racing, any time you're going up (or on the flat, for that matter) you assist by pumping rhythmically with one leg, the other leg on a runner, or by pushing with a ski pole, or both. When it's steep, you get off the sled and trot along with the dogs for as long as you can; and when you can't, which comes sooner than later if you're an old fart, you resume the pumping and pole pushing where you left off. In 2010 I will labor near the top in truly severe conditions, bunched up with Middie Johnson of Unalakleet, Swenson and Dee Dee Jonrowe, when I glance gee and see cabin lights. I glance again, and I *still* see cabin lights. I have never noted a cabin in the pass, and I've never been *told* of a cabin. It could be a hallucination, but I don't much care because I have my hands full keeping my team, and my mind, on the trail in the maelstrom of swirling snow. Later, at Rohn, Swenson will say the pass was the toughest he had ever seen it.

But it can be worse—a lot worse. In 1984 all the mushers will be advised to travel in pairs and to tow an avalanche cord. With recent warm weather and tons of moist snow, conditions are "ideal" for an avalanche. It occasions a person to think things over, like "What on earth am I doing here?" Soon what I'm doing is traveling right behind another team, and with a length of rope dangling aft. Those precautions feel like whistling in the wind, but we dangle through without any hint of a snowy burial. No Iditarod racer has ever, that I'm aware, been hit by the avalanche, but the same cannot be said of others. In 2008 Richard Strick, a trailbreaker from McGrath, will be swept away to his tragic demise. Mushers beware—and be thankful.

In 1979 I'm on the top of the pass, Iditarod's maximum elevation, in midday and in good weather. That top is marked by a cairn, and in time to come by a sign: "Rainy Pass. London this way, Fargo that…" (just kidding about Fargo.) The sign signifies that we're about to head down into the fabled, and feared, Dalzell Gorge. Although steep, the first part is no big deal, given good visibility and a discernible trail. This rookie is lulled into postulating, "It can't be so bad." But in 2009 I will start down in the dark, as is customarily the case, and in horizontally blowing snow, obscuring any trail markers not knocked down by previous teams. At any rate, I can't *see* any markers or anything past the front of the team and in no time am plummeting down the mountainside with utterly no idea where I'm headed. I recall, or conjure up, some cliffs in that region and feel like an extreme downhill skier, mushing to my doom in the white darkness. Somehow, I'm able to stop the team and drive the hook deep. It remains driven just long enough for me to get to my leaders. I don't know what I'm going to do and don't get to find out because when the team pulls the hook, I snatch the sled as it zips by, and we resume the blind, uncontrolled descent as before. This, I must confess, is one of my most frightening moments ever, and I think that's saying something. Fearing the cliff will claim me at any second, I do see a marker and, miraculously, we're back on the Iditarod Trail, about where in '79 I begin to strike an occasional rock.

Occasional, then less occasional, and the notion that it can't be so bad evaporates. With decreasing elevation comes decreasing snow, and increasing rock and ice. The sides of the gorge close in like a vise. Your team decides it's time to test your sled handling skills, and your resolve. Lurching downhill, you are slammed from one hard spot to the next and given ample opportunity to snag the increasing numbers of gnarly bushes and small trees. The worst is saved for the last when, after an hour or more of this exhausting roller coaster, you enter a region of varyingly stable ice bridges spanning the now sizeable and alternatingly open Dalzell Creek. Slanted sheets of glaciation and shelf ice are poised to suck you into the raging torrent, and it can happen.

Heading Down the Dalzell for the Less Occasional Rock

Shortly after the first rock, the trail (the correct, desired trail) runs along the top of a narrow ridge. No problem on the ridge, but big problem if you stray. Each side drops off sharply down to a creek, flowing mostly under the snow and ice, until you land on it and break through. None of this is even noticed by the fortunate who thread the needle atop the ridge and go onto seek their misfortunes elsewhere. I seek mine right there and will become intimately familiar with the alternate topography of the place. One year my leaders will choose the left side. By the time I get the team stopped and the sled anchored precariously, half my team is hanging off the ridge top with the leaders at the bottom, in the darkness and in the creek. Grasping the gangline, I give it a mighty tug, at the same time pleading vainly with my "front end" (front of the team) to come back up. They try, but when I hop down to them I discover why they can't. The snow in that hole is deep, and I sink in up to my waist. I can scarcely move, to say nothing of moving those dogs. It's time to stop and reevaluate. I do, and the solution comes to me. With effort, I shinny up the gangline to the sled (to my good fortune, still on the ridge) and pull a long piece of rope from out the sled bag. Then I hop back down to the errant animals, tie the rope to the leaders, and shinny back up. Now I have leverage. When I pull, the rope-assisted dogs are able to scramble up the snowy slope and regain the ridge top. Not much lost, except nearly an hour's time and sweat equity.

Another year, my leaders and then the entire team will opt for the *right* side of that same ridge. This time my whole outfit winds up at the bottom, the bottom of the right-sided ravine. The good news is that snow and ice are holding us above the rushing water below, for the present. The bad news, outweighing the good, is that two of my females are in heat. They are at the back of the team, hypothetically best, a la Rick Swenson. But in this situation, again, not so best because before I can hook down the front of the team, all the males seize an opening and execute a 180, coming fast to where the girls are. I am confronted by the inevitable and now familiar wad of balled-up, breeding, biting dogs. (Yes, I know what you're thinking, and I reckon I never *do* learn.) For some time I try to haul them up to the trail, but the slope is too steep, the snow too deep, the sled too heavy, and the dogs too preoccupied. I'm assisted in all this by Gerry Willomitzer, who risks losing his team by parking it up on the ridge and helping me. I am deeply thankful, indebted to him. Alas, though, our efforts are in vain, and Gerry must take off before another musher comes along, which happens—Robert Bundtzen, perchance. Whoever, he is able to stop before plunging all the way down to my low level. Finally, accepting that this time I will never regain the ridge, I reorganize the critters and then fumble on ahead, reconnoitering down the ravine to where its rock walls narrow to just over a sled's width and the iced-over creek cascades underfoot, but not for long. When the ice gives way I wind up on some slippery rocks in about a foot of rapidly moving ice water. Feet wet again, but that's the least of my worries. It's not even cold, a few degrees above zero. I don't know for certain, given my headlamp's limited range, but I fervently hope that below and once past the narrowing, we will be able to rejoin the trail. Such had better be the case because I'm about to put all my eggs in that basket, having no other choice, really. I scramble back up to the sled, release the hook from somewhere down by the creek bed, catapult down the ravine in the open creek as we thread the rocky gap over a precipice and then, incredulously, pop back onto the trail. Two hours off the clock this time, and drenched by sweat as much as by the water.

When your team gets balled-up in its lines, as above, and you commence the unballing, it is often necessary to unsnap some of the dogs, and it's way easy to end up with a loose one. All's well if the dog comes to you when called. If the dog thumbs its nose at you, however, the result can be a team member *in absentia*. This can be very disconcerting because of the race rule not allowing a musher to continue without all dogs at each checkpoint. Without all hands, or paws, you will be forced to scratch or will be disqualified. Such a stray dog is not uncommon, like when my friend, Gunnar Johnson, loses my dog Uma, as chronicled in his *Mushing Magazine* article, *Uma and Me*; and also when Newton Marshall loses our dog May in the 2013 Iditarod, initiating May's few hundred-mile pilgrimage home (and Newton's scratch, unfortunately). It will happen to me twice during my dashes down the Dalzell, but my most noteworthy missing mutt moment will will come to pass in 2004 when, just past my pet ridge, I meet a lone dog, a lone *white* dog trotting toward me, trotting backwards toward the pass and the prior checkpoint (Rainy). I recognize it as one of *my* white dogs, but not from my team. Anna, also in the race, has been moving out ahead of me (*well* ahead, actually), and she lost the dog. I attach it to the front of my sled and, abracadabra, I have a seventeen-dog team! Against the rules, but what can I do? Fifteen minutes later and there's Anna, happy to see me but more happy to see her missing mutt.

I come to think of Dalzell as requiring almost two hours, but that's in a good year, and I will have only a handful of those. 1979 is not good. "This is bad, real bad," I tell myself. How long can it continue? How long can *I* continue? The answer to the second question is *as long as IT continues*. Like the whole Iditarod, much of the time you are in lock step with everybody else, something akin to the wannabe gold miners on Chilcoot Pass in 1898. In lock step—up, down, around, over. Slam, bam, thank you Ma'am. Hit something, lose control, tip over, grip the sled until it grinds to a standstill in the roughness. I don't know how or where it happens, but by the time I hear the helicopter and see the film crew (BBC?) my sled doesn't handle worth beans because it is severely damaged. I hear Dick Mackey, with the film crew, ask me, "Jim, you okay?" "Yeah, I'm fine," I lie. Not long after that we've seen the worst of it, and we exit hell onto the Tatina River. Then, while struggling the last few miles to the Rohn checkpoint, often icy and gravelly but flat, I mull over my situation and ruminate on how I ever will manage to leave the checkpoint with my busted, unstable, essentially unusable sled.

Chapter Twenty-Five
BODY PARTS

We are at Rohn, a level and heavily wooded oasis on the South Fork of the Kuskokwim River, with closely-placed and good-sized trees providing ideal shelter from the cold wind sighing high above. A small Bureau of Land Management cabin, operation base for race officials, is also available to mushers. Space for sleeping is very limited, and the cozy conditions necessitate camaraderie and some degree of creativity. I will one day, or one night, be squeezed onto an upper bunk, snuggling with Martin Buser and some other guy's smelly feet. Such sleep as can be accomplished, Tang before the sleep, coffee afterward, and the thawing of your food as you attempt to dry your clothes are all more than welcome. But the best part is the stories told by so and so about so and so's race to date. It makes me appreciate that my troubles are not unique. One of the best Rohn stories is centered on Raymie Redington, Joe's son, who is said to have responded to a dare by taking several bites out of a skinned beaver carcass hanging on the wall.

Rohn presents me with a dilemma. A genuine sled builder with his repair kit is at hand, but race rules prevent me from requesting assistance. The solution comes after I drift off to sleep, having no idea how I'm going to fix my broken sled. In the morning I shuffle outside and am flabbergasted to see that it has been expertly repaired by a good fairy and is ready to ride. That sled builder has waved his magic wand, and all is well. I have not asked for assistance, and have not even had a chance to refuse it. At any rate, the Rohn race officials seem happy enough that I'm able to leave the checkpoint.

This chapter could be entitled *Beyond Rohn*, a subset of *Beyond Ophir*. *Beyond Rohn* lacks, however, most of *Beyond Ophir's* unknowns and uncertainties. What I mean is that travel Bey*ond Rohn* is *predictably* awful for the first three or four hours. Bumpy trail with minimal snow, ice, gravel, rocks, roots and stumps combine to provide another Rough Rider ride. In 2000 Anna will experience this to the nth degree. She gets through the Dalzell with one hand, the other fractured functionless, and she reaches Rohn thankful that the worst is over. I was not able to show her the rough trail Beyond Rohn, on our *one snowmachine*, and I minimized its rigors. So after her Rohn rest she departs, still one-handed but optimistic, only to meet up with the most horrible conditions and stop when she just can't take it any more at an inopportunely elevated, wind-swept spot. Anna tries to get her cooker lit, and then weeps silently. By this time she not only can't use her left hand, she has injured her right shoulder, possibly a dislocation. Partly because she cannot produce hot water for her dogs, she needs to get moving, and does so after about an hour. While descending onto a lake, for the second time she crashes into the wrong side of a tree. Along comes veteran musher Ed Iten, who helps reduce her *sled's* dislocation and swears they are only a short way from smoother sailing. Both the trail and Anna's outlook soon improve.

Another predictable, actually *predicted*, example will arise in 1999. At Rohn, we are all told that departure from the checkpoint is at variance with the norm because the river is open and flowing, and that we will cross it at the shallowest ford available. When I arrive at the ford, lead my leaders and wade in, I lose both my footing and my control of the dogs. Then there's more splashing through the water until I catch up and pull the dogs to the opposite bank. No harm done, and really not much time lost. Desiring some distance between me and the river, I take off straightaway, feet sopping wet, intending to run a short distance and then stop to change into dry socks and back-up boots. My booted feet, however, feel oddly rigid but otherwise okay, and I mush on, all the way to Nikolai, seventy tough miles and nine hours distant. It might have worked out, but the temperature at minus 40 dictates otherwise. Indoors, somebody assists with the removal of my solidly frozen footwear, and I remove my socks. Both the assistant and I are utterly revolted by a ghastly site. Seven of my frostbitten toes are swollen, red and blistered, and it is apparent that my right *big* toe is no longer part of Jim Lanier. Recipients of some first aid, the alien appendage and I get back on my sled and go on to conclude the race, 750 miles later.

After those miles and then many weeks, that toe and I part company when it is amputated. A tragedy, needless to say, and my friends and family react accordingly. Joan Bundtzen, my pathology partner and wife of musher Robert, examines the dead digit as a surgical specimen. Then she organizes a memorial service at which she intones *Ode to Toe,* with the deceased shriveled up like a prune, sporting a tiny tuxedo, and laid supine in a very small coffin. Mourners pen numerous sympathy cards with inscriptions as follows: "Well, as toes go, it won't be long now" and "When you lose someone special, it always feels like a part of you is missing...." Then from Thoreau, "Every blade in the field, every toe on the foot lays down its life in its season as beautifully as it was taken up."

Most moving is Joan's obituary:

Toe. Born October 28, 1940. Died May 21, 1999, of complications secondary to severe frostbite suffered during the Iditarod. Toe had a shy and retiring personality and was seldom seen by any but his immediate family and close friends. He will sorely be missed. He leaves behind his lifetime companion, Jim Lanier; close friends Anna Bondarenko and Jimmy Lanier; nine siblings and ten cousins.

Close friend Anna, an accomplished vocalist, intends to offer a memorial song, but she is thwarted by a malfunctioning automobile and arrives late, after the end of the service. The number she had selected, and altered, from Handel's Messiah, was *How beautiful are the toes of them....*

The Deceased
Photo Courtesy of Eagle River Photo, erphoto@mtaonline.net

Thereafter, toe will lie in his coffin, most presentably, and occupy a place of honor in my living room. His passing evens things up, to some extent. In 1984, early in the course of the Coldfoot Classic sled dog race in the Brook's Range, I made the mistake of pouring white gas on my funnel-grasping fingers, again at minus 40. The next day, at the village of Anaktuvik Pass, my fingers looked like my toes in Nikolai, with two totally alien fingertips. Requiring an assist just to open my fly, I stated that I would terminate my trip, but after forty winks and treatment prescribed by Dr. William Mills, a frostbite expert in Anchorage, I asked Joe May (Iditarod champ, 1980) if he would help me get started. Help he did, and I finished that race too, with the compromised hand in a large mitt the entire time. The funny thing, though, is that by Coldfoot's end the frostbite played second fiddle to exquisitely painful, bilateral (both feet) plantar fasciitis. I could hardly walk and had to be supported to get from my sled to a chair inside the Coldfoot truck stop, Dick Mackey, owner. So as I said, toe evens things up. Absent fingertips left side, the result of surgery by Dr. Mills, and absent big toe right. My friends, and my medical colleagues, like to kid me about disappearing as I mush along life's trail.

In 1979 I leave Rohn before Ron and drop down the riverbank onto a broad, mostly dry and very dark South Fork, featuring alternating sand, gravel, glare ice, driftwood and patches of willows. The dogs move well on the sand and gravel but find slippery going on the ice, *very* slippery since many are wearing booties. They cease moving forward and freak out, tiptoeing for the nearest gravel. Meanwhile, the wind treats the sled like a sail, and we are blown sideways, the brake like it's broken, ineffective on the ice. This ends when the sled slams suddenly into the gravel, or the driftwood, and tips over. Then I smart up, remove booties from the dogs' feet, and attach small crampons to mine. This facilitates progress, but I discover that markers, few for the race leaders, are by now nonexistent. In the gloomy darkness, I've only a vague notion where to go. My headlamp shows me a few abrasions in the ice, suggesting the prior passage of a dogsled, but after a mile or so, no more abrasions, nor nonexistent markers. I don't realize it, but I've gone past the point where I should have exited the river. We're running wild down what looks like the main channel with a tailwind pushing us hard and fast. I hear gurgling and glimpse gurgleward at a large, open hole in the river ice with the water surging, and I just miss it. I know I must stop, but when I stomp on the brake, we just sail by another open hole. At least we haven't sailed *into* a hole—not yet. I flip the sled on its side and sit on it, a maneuver that slows the team, but they don't stop until fair fortune shines as we gain some more gravel. Exhausted, partly by terror, I pause a few minutes to retrieve a facade of strength and will. Then I walk the dogs into a measured 180 and gingerly coax the team back onto the ice and into the wind, in the direction whence we've come. Into the wind and moving slower now, my headlamp provides a better view of the open holes. I shudder, and wish I hadn't looked. Having retraced our steps and back at the checkpoint, I wonder what became of Ron. I don't know how I missed him, but some time later he shows up, and we regroup to obtain better trail info. Ron recounts how, when he saw the open holes but not me, his foremost concern was how to explain my disappearance to my grieving family.

We wait for dawn, and second time's a charm. Off the river and back into trees, the trail is snow-poor and sporadically rooted, but almost a relief. It is here in 2004 that an indefinable form will take shape in the beam of my headlamp, in the trail and dead ahead. As the dogs nimbly hop over it, I brace for impact with the log, or whatever. Rather than "whack" we go "dull thud," almost "squish." I look back and see that it was, for heaven's sake, a moose, a dead moose. Wolf kill? Not much evidence for that, and no musher ever fesses up to a shooting, as far as I know.

Up, down and around for about an hour, and then Ron and I zip out onto the Post River and turn left. I don't know it, but in races to come the Iditarod will go straight *across* the Post and thence take a different route for the next twenty miles or so, to Farewell Lake. But in 1979 we turn left, as stated, and proceed *up* the Post. After a few miles on that river we exit right, off the river, and begin climbing up a mountain valley. The trail is good, the scenery spectacular. A pretty little mountain lake, Veleska, is without snow in places, and I gaze down through thick, translucent ice into the dark depths below. Very impressive, and a little disturbing. More climbing up a series of switchbacks, and then it's over the top of a divide. Ahead we view a long, broad, snowy expanse, summoning us down to distant trees, and down the expanse we go, to the Farewell checkpoint. Again, as with the bygone turn up the Post, Farewell will become checkpoint no more, but for now it provides the next place for us to dock our dogs. We are six days into the Iditarod, weather perfect, heads held high, moving steadily en route for Nome. All that will soon change.

Chapter Twenty-Six
LOWLIGHTS

B ut first, a return to the Post River. As I have indicated, in all my Iditarods after '79 the trail post-Post will be routed differently. It's an extension of that up, down and around, tough going prior to Post, but it introduces some notorious notables like the "Buffalo Tunnel" and "The Glacier." There is no question that in that region I will endure more hardship and trauma, more lowlights per mile, than in any other segment of the race.

1984, my second Iditarod, is the race in which I borrow Norman's team. For the first few days the weather, perfect in my first race, is atrocious with temperatures in the forties and rain, periodically heavy. The deep snow becomes soft and bottomless, accounting for that exasperating delay with Kansas, in heat on the Skwentna River. By the time I hit the trail out of Rohn, in all low spots the trail is full of water, small creeks have opened, and both lakes and rivers are awash in overflow, in some places two to three feet deep. The trail is often a pond, lined by trees on its shore. A driver of well-disciplined dogs, Susan Butcher, will tell me she had no pond problems, that her dogs trotted through confidently or marched around and moved on. Mine avoid the water like the plague and become tree huggers, making it necessary to literally pry them off, one dog at a time. Doing this means that I am repeatedly wading, which doesn't matter much because the constant rain has soaked me through and through. At one point we get into a deeper pond, possibly the result of earlier teams' breaking through the thinly iced-over surface. The sled floats, the dogs paddle, and I lurch forward while brushing aside big chunks of ice. Then looms a larger aqueous obstacle, the Post River, or conceivably a lake. (The exact location is up for grabs, as is much of that night.) The entire expanse is flooded, from shore to shore. Any markers have washed away, and I gaze out on dark, foreboding nothingness, my headlamp unable to illuminate the far side. For some unfathomable reason my critters rush ahead, as if sensing some kind of bearing. But then they become bearingless and are again swimming, requiring me to once more become lead dog in water up to waist deep. Forging forward, I alternate between scanning for even a faint suggestion of a shore and glancing aft at the dog-paddling team and floating sled, as wind-generated waves arch them leeward. Dreading my next step, I am suddenly gripped by fear when the rippling water strikes me as river current, or *is* river current, and I worry that the black ice under the overflow (and under me) may have thinned. "Don't let the fear paralyze you, Lanier," I say to myself. "Keep moving. There's no turning back." Another fifty yards, and my headlamp suggests a far bank. A few more insecure steps and yes, it *is* a bank, lined by bank trees. Some markers, like those on trees, bear reflectors, but no reflectors are to be seen. I have no idea where the trail is, or where it was. Nothing to do but slog forward. Then the overflow shallows, the dogs obtain footing, and the waterlogged sled no longer floats. I fasten the leaders to a bank bush and walk to the left. 50 yards, 100 yards. No trail. Back to the team, and to the right.. 50 yards.... and then I see it, a narrow chute from out of the water, up the bank and into the woods. I fetch the team, and they also see the trail and go for it, overjoyed as much as I to escape a watery grave on that inland sea.

Later that night I stop to afford my team some time to recoup, and we are joined by two other waders. With everybody and everything saturated by the unrelenting rain at 40 Fahrenheit, it is a recipe for hypothermia. After consuming some food, our animals appear remarkably comfortable, lying on some grass; but comfort eludes the waders, lying in the rain. Having agreed to stay put about four hours, we don't do that because the urge to get moving and try to warm our shivering bodies becomes overwhelming. It beats any temptation to lie down and let the cold take over. A few hours later the rain stops, the skies clear, and the temperature plummets to about minus ten. I try to change socks but cannot because one of my (bunny) boots has taken on water in its insulating space and is frozen, vise-like around my foot. It's not until Nikolai that I am able to set things right by removing the boot, with difficulty. For the next several days the thermometer hovers around zero Fahrenheit or lower, but there is still a lot of liquid water on the rivers. In Nome we will all be awarded a certificate, to wit: "...for swimming the Iditarod trail...."

Chapter Twenty-Seven
A CONTACT SPORT

I mentioned "Buffalo Tunnel" and "The Glacier." The "Tunnel" is named "Buffalo" because the region from Rohn to Farewell and beyond is the stomping grounds of the Farewell bison herd and because of a very narrow, tunnel-like segment of trail after the Post River, just before "The Glacier." The "tunneling" through a dense growth of small trees will just barely permit access by a team and sled, to say nothing of a buffalo! The tunnel is a real kick but begs a question: Would a buffalo like it as well, and might we meet head-on? It will not happen, nor will I come across a buffalo elsewhere. Other mushers will be more, or less, fortunate. A few will have close encounters of the buffalo kind, like Aliy Zirkle in 2001. It can be frightening and catastrophic, like the moose vs. wolf pack thing. (Bison brief: About another thirty miles past the tunnel comes "Buffalo Camp," a hunting outpost where mushers occasionally rest for a spell.)

That tunnel will become history when it is obliterated by a rockslide during the winter of 1997-1998, fortunately not during the race. The obliteration necessitates a new route, well to the side of the former tunnel. That it's no longer tunnel-like must be admitted, but the region retains the name. One thing will not change. At the end of the "tunnel" one erupts out of the trees into an open area, "The Glacier." More accurately, it's an incline that in most years is *glaciated* by water that turns to ice as it flows down the slope. Making it more interesting, a house-sized rock juts out from its right side and into its center. The best way up borders the rock, but the route is often poorly marked, markers being placed in ice with difficulty, and markers beyond the rock not visible *because* of the rock. This can be a very sticky wicket for a glacier rookie. My first time on that slippery slope, again in 1984, I will stop just before we are fully out of the tunnel and walk ahead to reconnoiter, in the dark, as almost goes without saying. (It seems axiomatic and perhaps logical that problematic places are so often in the dark.) As I return to my sled, another musher shows up behind me. When I hesitate, not sure what I'm getting into, Vern Halter, hot off his twenty-four in Rohn, asks for "trail" (meaning, "Let me get past, you slug.") The smart move would be to help Vern get by, and then let him lead me up the glacier. In lieu of smart, I stupidly pull the hook and hope for the best, but we are immediately in deep do-do. As Vern's team leaves the scene—to the right, up, around and to the other side of the big rock—*my* team, wearing booties, is slip-sliding away, the wrong way, to the left and *down* the glacier. The sled careens crazily as we pass a threshold and spin down into the abyss, or so it appears in that moment of dread, like we are falling off the edge of the known world. But no, the sled comes to rest at the natural terminus of the glacier, close to where the trail will arrive in future Iditarods.

A Problematic Place—How the Iditarod Trail Looks for Half of Every 24 Hours

Such farcical animal behavior is not confined to rookies. In 2010 it will happen to Ray Redington, Jr., grandson of old Joe or no. He will be running with Aliy

Zirkle who later tells the tale, quoting Ray's (expletive deleted) language as he and his team carouselled down the ice. Then again, in 2009, I will foolishly try the glacier's *left* side, up a near vertical embankment. My leaders attempt gamely to scale it, but with the ice, it's too much. It is the same year of that delay with those breeding bitches in the Dalzell, and my team is soon in another sexy snarl as we slide back down. This time a cameraman, primed for such a photo op, captures part of the mess on video. It makes me sick to watch it.

I always get by that glacier, some years easily, some not. Either way, things don't get any easier, not anytime soon. Right away comes a serious uphill, after which the trail levels off and then drops deceptively onto rock-solid, brown to black earth with virtually never any snow. The surface is uneven, unfriendly. At one point, if you are a touch too far off the mark, you go over a jump and can become airborne. This short, nasty part of the Iditarod is, for me, the roughest in the entire race, and the most damaging.

One year I will be in Rohn only long enough to grab some dog food and straw, and then head out with intent to camp after about two hours. I do camp, but first, as I bounce along and over that bumpy part, I hear the soft "crack" characteristic of a breaking aluminum sled runner. Soon afterward and sooner than intended, I stop, partly to see what I can do about the break. Later in that same race I will learn, of necessity when a second runner breaks, how to accomplish an acceptable repair. But at this time I don't do much and go all the way to Nikolai, on one runner and one leg.

Another year, as I fly over the "jump" in the rough part, I will indeed become airborne. My sled rolls nearly 180 degrees and lands on top of me, slamming my left side into the hard ground. Possibly unconscious for a moment, I become responsive to a searing pain in my left shoulder and a numbness in my left hand. I try to cry out, to nobody, but the wind has been knocked out of me, so I can't even produce a soft "woof." While I lie there until restored to a modicum of normal, I get my legs moving (a favorable sign), make a preliminary diagnosis of brachial plexus (nerve) injury in my neck and shoulder, and feel thankful that my sled augered into a hole and the team is still with me. Then another team comes flying down the uneven. It is piloted by Rick Swenson, the legendary five-time Iditarod champ, and he unaccountably shoots off into the woods. Once I begin to recover and get my house in order, I direct my headlamp at Swenson and bring to light another unhappy camper. I don't know if he caught air like me, but his outfit is undesirably strung out in the trees. As I go by I ask the customary, "You all right, Rick?" and Rick replies, "Yeah." That terse response might have been the same no matter how dire his predicament. That's just life on the trail.

Yet a third year, and I will be banging into those damn bumps when I stomp my left foot down, hard. I both feel and hear an ominous "pop." My initial impression is that it's nothing much, but then I realize that "This ain't good." After only another few hundred yards I see two teams at trailside, with both mushers watching my approach. I make them as Ray Redington and Tyrell Seavey, and one of them asks, "How you doing, Jim?"

"I may have broken my ankle."

"You'd better stop and check it out."

"No, I better keep going before it gels."

I do keep going, an unpleasant fifty miles or so to Nikolai. By then, the ankle is swollen and discolored—and gelled—and it hurts. I phone an orthopedic surgeon I know in Anchorage, the same surgeon who amputated my toe. His long distance diagnosis is a bad sprain, and he suggests I might keep on mushing, about what I wanted to hear. So I do just that, after spending my mandatory (for two reasons) twenty-four-hour pit stop in Nikolai. Riding the sled isn't too bad with most of my weight on my right leg most of the time. When the sled tips to the left, however, I can't compensate with my injured left leg, so we crash a lot, with additional damage to the ankle. Tending to the dogs at the checkpoints is painful and time-consuming, but I get the job done. The ankle *was* broken, *and* sprained, but I won't know that until several days after I hobble to Nome, 800 trail miles past the incident. I confess that's one time I should have withdrawn, in Nikolai, because that ankle will be recurrently stiff and sore 'til I limp my last. Oh well, like my frostbitten digits, it evens things up. Years earlier I busted my other ankle, again compliments of my sled dogs, thank you.

I'm not the only musher to damage things on that part of the race. Paul Gebhardt will hit something and sever his gangline in front of the sled, losing his entire team. And Zack Steer will impale himself on a stump and flee the race with a separated sternum. At the time of the '79 race Dick Mackey, perhaps with that post-Post region in mind, warned that inevitably someone would bash his brains out and become a sad statistic. It won't happen, at least not in the next thirty plus years, in all probability due less to mushers' fortitude and more to dumb luck. With Mackey's warning in mind and considering my own hard knocks, in 2009 I will start wearing hockey gear under my mushing clothes (chest, shoulder, elbow and knee protection) for the first 250 miles of the race. It makes me feel impervious, indestructible, and so far, so good, any false sense of security aside. For instance, in 2009 I take a tumble and literally bounce off that hard ground, unharmed. Without a doubt, and as iterated in Gunnar's *Mushing Injuries, a Case Study,* Iditarod is a contact sport!

Chapter Twenty-Eight
A FAREWELL TO CHARMS

Again consider our Farewell checkpoint, not far from where the once (as in 1979) and future new routes come together, having parted at the Post River. Ron and I reach Farewell as beneficiaries of a charmed race, so far, aside from difficulties in the Dalzell and just *Beyond Rohn*. The fair weather, slow but mostly steady progress and cheerful solidarity have perpetuated our Iditarod high. In this mind frame and hoping for furtherance of the same, inside a heated building I drift off comfortably, in a bed no less.

After a few comatose hours I discover that "It is not to be, Sherrie." Race charms are behind me. I get up, unsteady and nearly bowled over by the unexpected weakness. After lugging my reluctant body down a hallway and into a kitchen, I wolf down a bowl of soup and thirst for more. Despite having been told about the importance of drinking enough water, I have not, and dehydration has drained my reserves. Outside, Ron is preparing his team for departure. I join him and attempt the same, but my weakness overwhelms me to my knees. I encourage Ron to carry on alone, and I'm feeling mighty low as I head back inside to find more soup and shuteye.

When again stirring, the persistent weakness is accompanied by depression, and also by a paranoid delusion. All the mushers who have preceded me to Nome have lost their minds. They want me to drag my sorry self to race's end so that I will lose *my* mind. I can foil their plans by pulling out of the race, and that's precisely what I plan to do. With effort, I can concede that this is an opportune rationale, but it doesn't render the delusion any less real, or compelling.

A race official enters the room, and I tell him I'm scratching. He nods but points out that the weather has changed, with wind and a low ceiling. Airplanes for extraction of a scratched team will not be able to land at Farewell in the foreseeable. He says I might want to reconsider—*not* what I wanted to hear. By now my strength, but not my delusion, has improved, marginally. Ron, who did not leave but is waiting for me, offers to help. Tested by every effort and not sure of even Ron's intentions, I nevertheless accept his assistance with the packing of my sled and the bootying of some of my dogs. With me down and him up, I will come to value his help, and his encouragement. The opportunity to pay him back will arrive in due time.

Beyond Farewell come several lakes and a series of small hills. Round about twenty-five years in the future this part of the trail will have even less snow than usual, and in actual fact be snowless—bare, but not just bare—bare and *dusty*. When on each downhill one applies the brake or the drag, all is enveloped by a gritty, choking cloud of red dust. This is more than unwelcome, coming as it does after the snow-poor and funless passage through the environs of the "tunnel" and thereafter. Gritting and gagging through the dust, I meet a musher most unfortunate, a female rookie who is gimping along with an injured leg. I ask her how it happened. Another contact casualty, she replies that she lost control and banged into something. She protests bitterly about the trail that is not a trail, not the way a trail should be for a sled dog race, and lets on that she will never again commit the folly of entering the Iditarod. I've heard this from other rookies, as regards not only the Iditarod but other races as well, for example the Tustumena 200. In that race, after the first 100 miles of mountainous terrain comes a six-hour respite and then a repeat, backwards, of the original 100. During that respite, a rookie will pull in and complain, 'You couldn't pay me enough to go back over that (blankety-blank) trail!" Long distance sled dog races are not for the faint of heart, nor for whiners. That rookie with the leg issue will make her exit in Nikolai, her leg hurt badly enough, I'm sure. But I'll wager her psyche suffered more.

Following Ron in the darkness and in my weak, psychotic state, I am borderline cognizant of my surroundings. It's all I can do to remain upright, and I'm only dimly aware that we are entering the "Farewell Burn," an expanse laid waste in 1978 by the largest forest fire in recorded Alaska history. For mile after mile it's like a snowy, spooky moonscape, faintly illuminated by a partial moon through omnipresent clouds. Out of the hills, we're onto an interminably long flatland, devoid of appreciable vegetation except where punctuated by small oases of charred trees. By now the weather has further deteriorated—minus 25 with a wind quartering into my face. Often I can barely see my leaders, and at several points I worry that I've lost the trail. Relief arrives when I enter the next semi-protective, small stand of burned trees, but it vanishes as I exit to reface the numbing gale and uncertainty. Depression complete and my mood lowered even lower by fear, I have no choice but to hang on to the handlebar, lock-step on the treadmill, and ache for an end as my frigid fingers grasp for their grip. It's the beginning of a digital decline that will culminate in my amputated fingertips, six years in the frozen future. On the other hand, it's also the beginning of my learning how to get past the race's lows—that by definition, bad things will improve. It is the only way to learn this lesson, by bottoming out and persevering to the brightening dawn of another day.

Chapter Twenty-Nine
NIKOLAI

The flatland stays flat all the way to Nikolai. On this tabletop and into another cold wind, I will one day blink and ask, "What's the deal with my vision?" A nebulous dimness, it's happened to me a number of times. I close my eyes for a few seconds and my eyesight improves some. Ironically, Doug Swingley, at about the same time, is experiencing something similar, but his eyesight does *not* improve. Diagnosed with corneal frostbite, he is forced to pull out of the race and seek medical attention. The "cure" is prevention, which comes in two options. One, don't ever run the Iditarod—the safest and certainly the sanest, but so ordinary. The other, wear goggles or otherwise cover up your eyeballs. I have worn goggles, but I hate it. My preferred approach is to go barefaced and blink often early in the race. That way my nose gets numb and stays numb, painless, until Nome. Frostbitten of course, it turns red and then brown, but eventually it peels and heals for next year. Unlike fingers and toes, the nose goes good with frost, as does the face in general due to its abundant collateral blood supply. The opposite of collateral damage, this is desirable and advantageous, a supplementary and protective source of oxygen. Thus, frostbite of the nose or face, unless extreme, is self-limiting and works out just fine.

At about 4 AM we check in at Nikolai—cold, exhausted, dehydrated and banged up as usual. I realize that my paranoia pertaining to the other mushers might be delusional, but I can't shake it, and I'm still certain I should pull out. McGrath, another fifty miles with its direct flights to Anchorage, will be the place. My mind centers now on Nikolai, but even before I get checked in some guy runs rushes up and asks, "Are you Doctor Lanier?" I nod, and he relates a sad story. Earlier that day in Iditarod, almost 200 miles up the trail from Nikolai, a woman spilled a pot of boiling water on her breasts, as she was breast-feeding her baby. The baby was not harmed, but her breasts were boiled. Race officials knew of a doctor in the race, and word went out for me. (Why not for Doctor Ron or to Anchorage, I don't know.) Forcing my mind into medical mode, I prescribe whatever I can bring to that mind about burn therapy. "Two aspirins and call me in the morning" or something to that effect. Her condition could be critical, so I suggest she may need more treatment, as in Medevac to the recently opened burn (and frostbite) unit at Providence Hospital in Anchorage. This is loaded with irony, not only because I'm advising a burn patient on the trail, and not only because I have already incurred some frostbite, and not only because I work at Providence, and not only because the unit is new. It's also because a few weeks before race start some of my friends launched a Jim Lanier/Providence Hospital MUSH-ATHON. Thonic donors pledged pennies for each mile I would mush, with all proceeds to be credited to the new unit. My part is to go all the way to Nome so those donors will pony up maximum collateral through their collective noses. Now in Nikolai, I'm doubting that's going to happen.

As I respond to the inquiry regarding the boiled woman, a small crowd gathers round, comprised of local inhabitants. The Athabascan Indian hamlet of Nikolai is the first of the predominately Alaska Native settlements on the Iditarod. More than that, it is very familiar, very special to me because in the 1960s, while stationed at the Alaska Native Health Service Hospital in Anchorage, my wife and I made a few field trips to Nikolai, and to McGrath. We held clinics at which we examined patients and prescribed treatments, and we even spoke at town meetings. The people struck us as in need of a good many things, and my childhood First Methodist Church in Fargo, North Dakota, responded with heart-felt care packages. I relished those field trips, one of the highlights of my early days as an Alaskan, and it has served as extra motivation for participating in the Iditarod. That said, I turn to the crowd and recognize several people, many of them former patients. They're excited that their doctor has mushed a team of dogs all the way from Anchorage to make a house call.

Regarding houses, in these early years of the race each musher, after signing in at each checkpoint, resides at an appointed household (as opposed to everyone being "corralled" at the same prearranged locale, as will be the practice eventually). So, after homecoming handshakes, hugs and grins all around, my team and I go with a guy along village byways to his small, wood-framed dwelling place. My host graciously provides hot water, and I gratefully use it to prepare meat and fish for my puppies. Then I go inside and take pleasure in the aroma—nostalgic always—of wood smoke and moose stew. Those folks, Jeff and Doris Stokes, do everything to put me at ease, and I must confess that it brightens my mood a little. Some of the Nikolaians become friends, especially Nick and Oline Petruska, and I will visit them many times in the Iditarods ahead.

Chapter Thirty
THE PATH TO McGRATH

Nikolai is cold—still twenty-five below zero—and windy, imparting a very chilling chill factor. As we ready to leave, I am offered an encouragement. A local tells me the wind will be at my back, not in my face as was the case prior to Nikolai. I'm not sure I can believe it. This local could be part of the conspiracy. But in a little while I'm out on the trail, and the wind *is* at my back. I feel better, but not for long. As luck would have it, the wind wanes, but as bad luck would have it, the thermometer plunges to forty below. The fifty-mile run to McGrath, the next checkpoint, is most times easy with river, swamp, a few small hills and a smooth trail. This first time, though, it *ain't* easy. It's hard. Not just hard as in difficult, but as in steel, cold steel. North of the Alaska Range in Alaska's Interior, the trees are smaller, scrubbier, spookier and, yes, "harder" than in South Central where I live and train. This hardness—a new, sudden, sobering concept—hits me like a freight sled. It weighs heavy on my mind, and my depressed delusion recurs, as if it ever left. It must weigh heavy on the sled too, because I have the impression that we are hardly moving, but after several hours lights appear as we glide down a long, rightward sweep of the Kuskokwim. It's McGrath, one of the more sizeable communities visited by the race. Up the riverbank we go and then…where's the checkpoint? Damned if I know, so I take off down a snowy street. At 2 AM no one is streetside to ask for directions, and we zoom aimlessly from one end of town to the other. I say "zoom" because the lights, stray dogs and stray dog scents have piqued my team's canine curiosity to the max. Reinvigorated, they move at double time. It's kind of cool but frustrating because I'm depressed and I NEED TO FIND THE CHECKPOINT! At length, adjacent the airport, I guess the goal might be close. It is, and I'm there.

McGrath—Blue like Me

We are led to a building, also adjacent the airport, and I see that another of my dogs is favoring a front leg. I examine the leg and detect a sore shoulder. After massage with an ointment, I dress her in a warming jacket and hope for recovery. She should have plenty of time because I still intend to quit. After I feed the dogs and tend to other chores, I feed myself and pass out—on the floor.

For several hours I'm comatose again. Then it dawns on me that I'm in the Iditarod. Too bad, I must get out. Rummaging around, I locate a telephone, the first in more than a week. Desiring to pack my bags, I call home, seeking sympathy and the expected concurrence with my desiring. My wife answers. After the "Finally, we hear from you!" and "I've been worried," and "How are the dogs?" I ask her the question. "How do I sound?" "Not too bad, considering." How can she say that? It is an effort to speak, and she says "Not too bad?" Then I hazard the big one. "Should I scratch?" Her answer will ring in my ears for years. "Absolutely not! Too many people are counting on you, have pledged those pennies for you. The phone's been ringing off the hook, and you'd better keep going (because you'll never do this race again!)" There is no hiding from a wife's chiding, so I know I will indeed be getting out, out of McGrath—by dogsled and back on the trail. Not right away, since Ron and I are committed to our twenty-four-hour rest, but bailing out of the race is no longer an option.

For days I have dreamed of a beer at McGuire's Tavern. McGrath and that tavern at last, but the beer's allure has diminished. Tales of its abuse by some wayward mushers may have dissuaded me. I daresay some of the race's outcomes have been determined right here, by two or three 24's in succession. I will admit, though, that it has more to do with my exhaustion and mental state that I lounge around some ten to twelve hours *before* visiting McGuire's since I'm just surviving, in contrast to competing. It's not that I can't *find* the tavern. I've been there before, most recently in 1978, and besides, I can see it from my abode. In due course I do go inside and take a seat at the bar. The beer, while tasty enough, is not nearly as fulfilling as I'd dreamed it. Whatever is? But it's okay. Life's dreams—our hopes, our expectations, our scheming. That's the main thing. We persevere to the actual doing mostly to validate the dreaming, like I run the Iditarod to legitimize the pleasure of planning for the next year.

Flash forward to 1991. My young pal and protégé, Gunnar Johnson, will be off on his own Iditarod Odyssey. Having ridden the whip sled behind him to Knik Lake, I hop on a snowmachine and go as far as Skwentna. The trail surface is very abrasive due to recent freezing rain, very wearing on the booties that prevent the sandpaper-like ice from sanding the dogs' paws. I come across Swenson, stopped trailside to reboot because his dogs' footwear has been worn completely through. Delighting in his own inimitable self, Rick pokes fun at my modus operandi, by snowmachine, and scoffs that it looks so appealing and that he should switch to it.

Back in Anchorage, on TV and on the street, the buzz is that the mushers are out of booties and are in dire need of resupply. Many people respond, as to a call for a rare blood type. Fretting about Gunnar and his dogs, and responding to a self-serving obligation to spend more time on the trail, I plan to resupply him personally. I book airline passage to McGrath and take off, booties in hand. My arrival time should be perfect because Gunnar is about due. One, two, three hours pass, and no Gunnar. Another team shows up and relates that he espied a very sad Gunnar Johnson, not able to move and camped about thirty miles back. That's all I need to hear. Sergeant Preston to the rescue! After commandeering a snowmachine, I'm on my way; and after thirty of the fifty miles to Nikolai, there he is, a soundly sleeping lump in his sled, with a soundly sleeping dog team. All aglow in the luminescence of a full moon, the scene is dreamlike, but not for long.

"Gunnar, what gives?!"

"Jim, it's you! Thanks for coming. My team's quit on me. Can't get 'em going."

"Nonsense, Gunnar. Get out of the sack, and line out your critters!"

And so he does, but fifty yards later his critters seek slumber again. Painfully, I empathize with his despair and tell him not to worry, that "I'll be back" with a remedy. Sounds like crazy overkill, but I hop on that snowmachine and reverse course, all the way back to McGrath. Well past midnight I seek out a storeowner who lets me into his establishment where I purchase a belt and some bells. (Unlikely enough, neither Gunnar nor I had either.) In just over an hour I'm back at the moonlit scene. Unknown to Gunnar, my dogs revel in response to certain sounds, like the crack of a belt, or the tinkling of bells. They not only get going, they get going fast. "Jim, I like it!" shouts out a rejuvenated Gunnar as he cracks and tinkles in front of me, all the way to town. He won't like it for very long, but that's another story, best told by Gunnar himself. Weeks later, at a party in Anchorage, I will present him with a commemorative trophy, on which a plaque bears this limerick.

ON THE PATH TO McGRATH

An Iditarod musher named Gunnar,
whose dog team blew up, what a bummer.
He thought it was over
when exhausted old Rover
laid down, as to wait for the summer.

But for Gunnar, a lucky young man,
his mentor concocted a plan.
With a belt and a bell
all his dogs pulled like hell.
Down the trail, on to Nome, they all ran.

Chapter Thirty-One
BEFORE BEYOND

My gimpy gal has improved, and I'm packed and ready to mush out of McGrath. Ron Gould, bless his little ol' laid-back heart, is still with me and is still up, to my down. We've put in our twenty-four hours, or more, but no one's counting. At or near the back of the pack, the tail end of the Iditarod, no one is paying us a lot of attention. In years coming up the back of the packers will often be pressured to *get moving or you'll be gobbled up by the big storm that's coming* (or go home because we need to shut down the checkpoint so we can make the banquet in Nome). The banquet aside, and also aside that it may be a function of budget constraints, being last will be no fun at all. I always advise rookies, therefore, to stay a minimum of one checkpoint ahead of the last team, like one step ahead of the tax collector, or the mortician, or the *Mushing* Mortician (Scott Janssen, a rookie in the 2011 Iditarod). In these early days of '79, however, no one cares if we are at the back, or if we are competing, or if we live or die?

It's the strangest thing. Almost as soon as the lights of McGrath are extinguished by the river's bend, my attitude improves. Resigned to divine providence, perhaps, I think I may pull through, those veterans who want me to lose my mind notwithstanding. We glide o'er a frosty bog, and then decelerate. Fresh off our twenty-four in McGrath, my team at first moved smartly, but now *so slowly*. For nearly an hour I can't fathom what's happening, and then it hits me. We're going uphill, imperceptibly, so that it seems "on the level." This epiphany is confirmed after the high point, as we start down the other side. Being a bit "slow on the uptake" may be a manifestation of lingering mental incapacity, but I don't care. For the first time since Farewell, I feel terrific! And you see, that is inherent in the race to Nome. As Gunnar will say, you run through "the full range of human emotions," from the depths of despair to the heights of ecstasy, and frequently all in one day, or even one run. A more level ride might be preferable, but the depths can be (and are) repressed, and the highs are worth the price of admission.

A few more easy miles and we're in Takotna—a hop, skip and jump (18 miles) from McGrath. Only 18 miles, but since it's the next checkpoint, time for a break! Gould's rule. The place is lovely, with a wind-sheltering hill and trees, all overlooking the lazy, sinuous Takotna River. It will become mushers' top choice for their twenty-four-hour rest. With a windless tether for your dog team, a quiet church sanctuary for your siestas, 24/7 hot water, 24/7 steaks, 24/7 homemade pies and more (You order it, they cook it.), it takes more will power than I possess to deny myself a few hours in Shangrikotna.

There with Ron, we both eat and siesta well, not in the sanctuaried serenity of the church, but in slumber sound enough. Stewing over my gimpy gal, I keep her in the team because the next stop, the fabulous Ophir, is only 23 miles down the pike. On a road to a mining region, also to peoples' getaways, it's an easy run, smoothly uphill at first and very picturesque. Here one can succumb to another false sense of security, as in what can go wrong? It is the lull before the storm.

But first, Ophir, before *Beyond Ophir*. It's just a wide spot in the trail, bedecked by trees and featuring a cabin, built, owned, and occupied by Dick Forsgren, Ophir's perennial checker. The cabin and its inhabitants are gracious and congenial, too "mush" so as weary racers try to sleep, proximate to card games and other frivolities. The situation will be alleviated by the construction of a musher cabin, replete with bunks and a stove for heat. In 2007, in contrast to some of us who are resting in that cabin on our twenty-four, Lance Mackey passes by on his way to Iditarod, and on his way to his epic first Iditarod victory. Reacting to Lance's passing, Jeff King remarks, "There isn't much stop in that guy."

So what do Ron and I do in Ophir? You guessed it. We take another break. I cannot overstate to what extent our adventurous exploit is the antithesis of a race, the antithesis of all my races before me. In those upcoming Iditarods there will at all times be a push born of the desire to compete, to move as fast as possible. After all, it is the Iditarod Sled Dog *Race*, as in the Webster definition, "a contest of speed." And so, appropriate for a *race* and as expected of a *competitor*, I will *speed* along as *speedily* as I can manage. It is still strange that my first (non-racy) trek to Nome is (and will remain, I'm sure) the most grueling but, paradoxically, the best race of them all.

Ron Gould and Team, on the Break in Ophir

Part III

Chapter Thirty-Two
BEYOND OPHIR

It is a step into the unknown, in both a literal and a metaphorical sense. Not completely unknown because two years earlier, in 1977, the race was for the first time routed *south* after Ophir—the "Southern Route," over 300 miles from Ophir to Kaltag. In order come the villages of Iditarod (in truth, a ghost village), Shageluk, Anvik, Grayling, Eagle Island (a tent city, after the race's early years) and then Kaltag. The "Northern Route," about 20 miles shorter, frequents Cripple (another tent city), Ruby, Galena, Nulato, and Kaltag. In all future races the southern route will be for odd years, the northern for even. This provides some variety, inviting varied race strategy and local participation (plus, it must be said, a breather).

Beyond Ophir is not completely unknown to my companion, Ron, since he made it as far as Iditarod on his first attempt in 1977, before being stymied by a snowstorm and the consequently obliterated trail. As we leave Ophir and take the left turn toward Iditarod, away from Cripple, it has not dawned on me that Ron's failure in '77 might be weighing heavy on him as we head into the land of his undoing.

It becomes obvious that there's not much *Beyond Ophir*, except miles and miles of nearly uninhabited and trackless wilderness. I say "nearly" because of the Iditarod every other March, but otherwise just wild country, wonderfully wild country. We slip through it soundlessly, except for the soft hiss of the runners, the dogs and their musher awed into silent reverie. Even the trail itself becomes wild, minimal, with no more roads and only a sporadic marker. This bliss is interrupted by a ceaseless side-hilling, threatening to suck the sled off into deep snow as we seem to parallel a river along the canted shoulder of a river valley. The end of the valley, and of the side-hilling, coincides with the end of the small, scrubby spruce. We see we will head up into a high, open vastness known as the Beaver Mountains. Mindful of what that could bring, I say to myself, and to my team I suppose, "Oh, no!" Trees, even scrubby ones, offer shelter from the wind, so before leaving them we declare yet another break, albeit a short one this time. After feeding my animals I walk over to Ron and ask, "How's it going?" No reply, which is uncharacteristic. About to rephrase, I'm stopped by his countenance. Something is amiss. Whether due to worries involving what lies ahead or to his lurking depressive disorder (which will become fully expressed in a few years) or to both, I can't say. But right now, Ron is singin' the blues. The cloud that hanged so heavy over my head now dissipated, I'm up, and he's down. Reciprocating, it is my turn to take care of Ron Gould, or at least to understand.

Singin' the Blues

The Beaver Mountains, End of Trees

Vastness

In less than an hour we pack up and move out. Bereft of trees, uphill we go, up into rolling, wind-swept tundra, as far as the eye can see. In daylight, we can pick our path well enough, with a moderate wind serving notice as to how things could be worse, that they *will* be worse. Off to one side is a herd of caribou, running effortlessly over the rugged ground and gliding like a hovercraft, an astounding sight. There is not much snow, so we slide on withered weeds and bounce off the rock-hard tussocks. One year there will be no snow whatsoever, and the sled will go "bang, bang, bang" as it hits a tussock every few feet for 70 miles, all the way to Iditarod. What torture! You get off the sled and try to run, which becomes undoable as the dogs go faster with your derriere off the runners.

Can You See the Caribou? (or just the tussocks)

Times passes, and finally both darkness and the trail descend, down off the mountain plateau and back into trees. Heavenly trees, a musher's delight, even if the wind is not winding because winding it might; even if the cold is not colding because get colder it might; and if colder, want the cheery warmth of a wood fire you might. We make camp at the site of the future Don's Cabin, also at the site of Don himself. Explanation? Don Montgomery, an insurance company guy from Ohio, is in this race, and now we chance upon him. He is living, and suffering, his dream—to someday see Nome. Like so many, including yours truly, he is discovering that it's not so easy. Don will never again run the Iditarod, but instead will appropriate some funds for a cabin to be built right where he is now. I took him into account earlier, around Rohn. He had a fast team then and got ahead of Ron and me. Now, his fast team having slowed, he hopes they can continue at any pace. Don comes across about the same as the team—slowed, as the trail's grim realities have set in.

Descent into...

...Trees...

...and Darkness

Gould and I start to fire up our Coleman stoves but have second thoughts when we espy some wide, deep craters in the snow, residues of wood fires burned by mushers now far ahead of us. All along the wilder stretches such craters may be noted (in the Iditarod's earlier years). In next to no time we are melting snow to boiling water over the burning branches. It's faster than a Coleman and a lot warmer—that cheery warmth--a very worthwhile bonus at the present minus 30. Once the pot is full and steaming, we empty it into a cooler full of frozen meat and fish. After the meat and fish thaws and the resulting stew cools (Dogs won't eat it if it's too hot.) we add some kibble (dry dog food), ladle it out into dishes and serve it up to the puppies. Not to my gimpy gal, though, because she did not improve enough to continue, and I left her in the care of the vet at Ophir, from there to be flown back to race start. The other twelve dogs all curl up on the straw I've carried from Ophir and are soon sound asleep. But not Ron and I, not for some time. We are tending to their feet and other body parts, as well as patching up equipment and readying for our inevitable departure. Then at last we spread our bags in the sleds, shed boots and some clothes, and get in. Sleep is immediate, but brief.

A Crater

Creating a Crater

Two more mushers show up, so we're not at the very tail end of the race, but darn close. These other two are Harry (or "Hairy," with cause) Harris of Nome, and Gene Leonard. That's five of us, briefly together at that future Don's Cabin. There is no way to foresee it, but from here on we five will remain together, at least in the checkpoints. Inspired by Jerry Riley, some people will take to calling us "The Executive Camping Party," although only Don Montgomery might have merited such a moniker.

Chapter Thirty-Three
ON TO IDITAROD

True to the notice served in Chapter Thirty-Two, things do worsen with a "freshening" of the wind, only moments after we leave "Don's." The miles ahead can be tiresome, even boring, but not this time. We step through an overflown creek, resulting in wet boots, cold feet and a change of socks, unfortunate timing since we just got started and have fifty miles to go. Much of the fifty is again high and exposed to the gale, which is now creating a whiteout and making navigation very challenging. We can't see much, rendering almost useless the very few upright markers not taken out by the wind and the sleds of prior teams. As in Rainy Pass, we slam into and over the wind-generated sastrugi as we search for the trail, our headlamps piercing the darkness, probing for those sled-generated abrasions in the hard-packed surface. Ron and I are now close together so when one goes awry, the other can hope to pick up on the error and right the wrong; but it usually means that *both* of us go wrong and get lost, and get lost we do, over and over. After slogging along, or crabbing down a hillside, we can no longer discern any allusion to a trail, only darkness and the howling of the wind. At that point we have three choices. First, forge ahead. I don't think so. Second, turn around and backtrack until we identify something. Effective, but so discouraging (also too sensible, too much like your wife's "Why don't you just ask for directions?"). And third, leave the teams and walk right, then left, the same procedure as in the overflow, with a faint trail emerging eventually. Then, desperate to relocate the teams, dead-reckon back in their general direction, on the hillside, in the darkness, through the whiteout and often aided by much shouting, even screaming over the tempest's roar—for Ron, or for Jim. In similar circumstances mushers can fail in such a search, spending the night in a snow cave or other shelter until relocating their outfit by dawn's early light.

Before gaining Iditarod, that right/left procedure we all but perfect, repeating it numerous times and making for much apprehension, frustration and slow going. People often ask if I've ever been lost. With this game of hide and seek continuing the next night, and the next nights, to answer two or three dozen times is no exaggeration.

With all that, it takes more than ten hours to travel the fifty miles to Iditarod, but at long last the race's namesake becomes visible around a bend in a slough. The "town" is not much to look at, not much if *not* looked at, just a very few old, dilapidated, grizzly-grey buildings—ghostly remnants of its long ago days of glory when nigh unto 10,000 souls patronized its gold assayer's office, mercantiles, livery stables, dog barns, brothels and saloons, and heard "some talk of building a church" (Twain). *We* hear some talk of heated tents, erected by a Boy Scout troop from one of the villages. Their quarters look very inviting, but we are not invited. The Scoutmaster informs us that race officials only, not mushers, are allowed to sleep in the tents. Rebuffed, Ron and I shiver into our sleds at minus 30.

The year-round population of Iditarod is currently (1979) about six, a family consisting of a man and wife, their kids and a baby. A few years ago they settled into this "end of the river" outpost, having tried to avoid

Iditarod, 1979

More of It, or What's Left of It

Off Limits to Mushers

any vestige of civilization, rejecting all the established Yukon basin communities. With the race passing through every other year, they now feel crowded and are considering relocation to a homesite more remote. The word *Iditarod* is said to mean "a far place" in the indigenous Native American dialect. Not far enough for some.

Inside their cabin, Iditarod's only habitable structure, the man of the house is feeding the baby, his wife nowhere to be seen. It turns out that his wife, the baby's mother, is the woman of the boiled breasts, about whom I was queried back at Nikolai. She *was* Medevac'd to the new thermal unit and is reported to be doing well. I can report Dad as likewise, if slightly overwhelmed. After a good-natured verbal exchange, during which I fess up to being their mama's radiophone doctor, I bid them adieu and go back outside.

The Man and the Baby

I will never have an easy run to Iditarod. It's too far, too daunting. But one time, it will be downright amusing. With only a short way to go, I'm treated to an amazing, almost comical sight: bicyclists, pedaling sluggishly through the snow, on their bicycles and on their way to Nome. Appearing pained, they stammer, "How far to Iditarod?" but less pained when I answer, "No more than five miles." Not long afterward, when talking to Sonny Lindner at the checkpoint, I say, "Sonny, did you see those guys on the bicycles? And people think *we're* crazy!"

Chapter Thirty-Four
ONE GOOD GOULD

Depending on trail conditions and fifty-seven other things, reaching Iditarod can be gratifying, accomplishing, thrilling, life-saving, historic, winning (Lance making his move), comic (as in bicycle) and so on. One thing it always is—halfway to Nome, the sobering recognition of which often hits hard in the fragile psyche of a rookie, as it does me in '79. Close onto two weeks, it seems an eternity I've been on the trail, that otherworldly separation from life, that separation so pervasive that one exists only for the next checkpoint, the next hill, the next bend in the river, the next pawprint in the snow. It will seem an eternity twofold by the time I reach Nome.

The Executive Camping Party, not yet any kind of real entity, is by happenstance in Iditarod all at the same time, but without any deliberate intent of traveling together. Ron and I leave the checkpoint, not sure where the others are, not sure of anything except that we're into some very big hills. Up, up and up some more, off the sled jogging and pushing, exhausting our dwindling energy reserves while working like the dogs and sweating like pigs, I should have removed a layer or two but am glad I didn't on the next long downhill in the frigid air. After one of those downhills I stop to wait for Ron, who has fallen back. Angrily pulling up to me, he scolds, "Of course you know by now, Jim, that going so fast downhill is what injures dogs. I really don't want to be detained when you need to tote a couple dogs in your damn sled!" Now fact is, in my opinion, I have not been going too fast, and Ron's team has been slower from the start. Fact also is that Ron is still blue, and getting bluer. Previously manifest by a stoic silence, his blueness has spilled out in that condescending criticism, possibly spawned by the rigors of the hills. Knowing Ron as one good Gould, kind and funny, if at times manic in his funniness, I write off his comment as an aberration born of depression and reply with a "You don't know what the f___ you're talking about…but I'll slow down," or something along those lines. Those are the first contentious words uttered between us, and the last—remarkable, considering the circumstances.

Halfway to Shageluk the terrain begins to level out, becoming gently rolling, finally almost flat. I will one year be moving along acceptably but drowsily when I dream up one of mushing's nightmares. Actually no dream but a sickening reality, my team suddenly lengthens, the front two thirds separating from the rear. Puzzling for a few seconds, it then hits me that the gang line has unraveled, leaving the sled with only four dogs pulling and me pushing. Horrified, I watch the front eight critters pull away. I'm moving at half-speed, with another twenty miles to the checkpoint. Lucking out, we catch up to the runaway dogs, ensnared by bushes, my prayers answered. Straightening out the disordered but uninjured animals plus emergency splicing of the gangline accomplished, we are on our way again—in one piece, one gangline, and one gang.

In Shageluk for about eight hours, we have time to conduct a cursory survey with exploration of our temporary digs, the village school. It's a brand new "Molly Hootch" school. A court decision stemming from litigation on behalf of a schoolgirl named Molly Hootch and others provided funding for construction of new schools all over bush Alaska, and thus the school's somewhat whimsical name. Outside the school, I take a picture of two kids, two "Shagelukians."

Their Molly Hootch School in the Background

The Shageluk Checkpoint with Gene Leonard and His Boozehounds

The next pit stop is Anvik, reached via 27 miles of swampland, mostly. In a future race there will be little snow and lots of brown, dry grass flanking the trail. My dog Uma, who has a penchant for trouble as experienced in spades by my old friend, Gunnar Johnson (*Uma and Me*), is up to her old tricks. Sniffing out browner pastures, she wriggles out of her harness and then curls up in the grass. Other dogs follow suit and sniff their way to the grass as well. Soon the entire team is settling in. Once begun, this rebellious behavior is replicated several times, causing me much consternation and delaying our arrival in Anvik by at least an hour.

Anvik is a charming little burg tucked into the shore of the mighty Yukon. It is said that the first team is greeted by the ringing of village bells. That I may never confirm unless I can accomplish the first team feat, which I will do in 2012, but not at Anvik. It will be for the halfway prize at Cripple checkpoint on the race's Northern Route. That prize is a really nice marble-based trophy, plus $3,000 of gold. When presented with my winnings I am asked what I will do with it, and I answer that it will no doubt wind up hanging from my wife's neck (the gold, that is). True to prediction, next Christmas Anna will receive a necklace featuring a silver pendant on which is embedded a dog's paw with pads of gold—the halfway gold from Cripple.

The Golden Paw
Courtesy of Abbie McMillan, New Hope, Minnesota

As to the bells of Anvik, Linwood Fiedler will one day confirm their greeting and report hearing the ringing as an almost religious experience. Besides bells, the other thing to greet the intrepid Linwood will be a seven-course gourmet meal, catered in Anvik by Anchorage's Millennium Hotel. Greeting Ron and me is a single tired checker, clipboard in hand to register the name, rank and serial number of our dog teams. Someday I'd like to eat that meal, and hear those bells.

Anvik

We go through Anvik and head back out onto the Yukon, on which river we will mush for the next 150 miles. It goes north, into the prevailing north wind, with today being no exception and prevailing at around 25 miles per hour. With the ambient temperature below zero, it's a prescription for a real ordeal, ameliorated to some degree by a facemask and by standing backwards on the runners. Still, it's cold!

Thirty years hence my team and I will part company on the river after Anvik. I'm moving in an uncomplicated fashion, so uncomplicated that I fall not only asleep but off the sled, to be jarred awake when I land in the snow. The dogs motor on without me. Then comes the automatic and futile "Whoa!" and the short jog, followed by the increasingly familiar Iditarod plod, toward Grayling, fortunately no more than five miles distant. Also fortunate, along comes another musher, Cim Smyth by name. Cim says, "Hop on," and together we give chase, tugged along by his strong team, as mine recedes into the horizon. This time I have lost my dogs on the Yukon with no bushes to snare them, and without another team to snare them. I can only hope they turn off the river and into the checkpoint, as against continuing on to Eagle Island, another seventy-five miles. Not knowing what's become of them until we turn into Grayling ourselves, I am relieved to see my dogs all laid out in regulation fashion and looking like, "Where you been, boss?" Later I'm being interviewed by a newspaper reporter who asks, "After your unorthodox arrival here, what are your plans now, Jim?" I counter with, "Heck, I'm going home. Those dogs of mine got here by themselves, even checked in just fine without me. I know when I'm not needed."

Chapter Thirty-Five
THE RUN FROM HELL OR NOT

Now in Grayling, the Executive Camping Party has coalesced into a disputably cohesive unit. We are gathering in the checkpoints, reviewing the previous run, the run from hell or not, telling lies about how we dealt with hell or not, and projecting the next episode of hell or not. The latter assumes a standard format, that of Gene Leonard leaving first, and the balance of our band later. Gene's booze hounds are so slow that even spotted an hour or more, he will arrive at the next checkpoint after the pokiest of the others in our little pack, having been passed by everyone en route. We get to feeling sympathetic for Gene, so much so that we take to preparing his dog food for him, allowable since a musher, and only a musher, is permitted to help another musher. Then Big Gene will show up, red-cheeked and frosted over, like "a miner fresh from the creeks, dog-dirty, and loaded for bear" (*The Shooting of Dan McGrew*; Robert Service). Gratitude-bound not to tarry, he goes straight to his work, determined to get underway without delaying us more than necessary. His first act is to replace his damp shoe packs with dry ones, for the elusive warmer feet on the next run. After joining in for a brief chat, he catches an equally brief nap and is off. One tough cookie that guy, the quintessential sourdough. I don't know how he keeps going.

I'm farmed out to the home of Grayling's Mountain Deacon. He and his family take good care of me, providing not only a roof over my head and a comfy corner for my mutts, but also that again-so-nostalgic aroma of wood smoke and moose stew. On the way to the Deacons' I get a pretty good look at Grayling. Like some other villages, it reminds me of a snowbound town in New England, with steepled churches and scenes t'would inspire a Robert Frost poem; and that's extraordinary because I've never been to New England.

Grayling

Mountain and His Deacons

Our visit in Grayling over, we gear up to make our exit, which means that Gene Leonard makes *his* exit, handicapped by the shortness of his sojourn. One to two hours later the four other party members remove toward the next watering hole, less than enthused about leaving such an enchanting hamlet. In the village we only *heard* the wind, somewhere high overhead, but out on the open Yukon it hits head-on, prompting redonning of the face masks, the shoring up of all flesh-exposing defects in our outer pants and parkas, and the resumption of the face-saving backward stance on our runners. The chill factor is rumored at minus 60, and it rumors numbingly for all of the next ten hours to Eagle Island, except that after sundown the cold intensifies. This might sound bad, but it gets worse. Approaching midnight, we are also approaching the time when humans are programmed to become drowsy. So drowsy we become, the drowsiness not desirable but unavoidable, like that when driving a car, fought futilely and for hours. The fight is worse than it sounds, and then sound itself encroaches. Hallucinations, reported by many Iditarod mushers, are mostly auditory, as opposed to visual. More often than not, my hallucinations take the form of a voice off to the side of the trail, and I answer involuntarily with a curt response, a "Yeah" or "What?" I'll tell you what, and what's worse. It's shooting a furtive glance in the voice's direction, becoming momentarily unbalanced, then stabilizing and realizing in an instant that no one is there. It does not, however, make the sound any less real. The combination of dozing and hallucinating wears a person down to a nubbin, to be revived only by a star-like check point light when it comes into view around a bend in the big river.

Man's best friend is truly a marvel, the sled dog variety manifesting its all but mythical ability to run, and run and run and run. But sled dog marvels don't end there, another ability most marvelous being the huskie's sixth sense for "sensing" things like checkpoints. As a comparatively senseless human being, I require that light to become aware of the checkpoint ahead, and on some occasions even the light doesn't rouse me. In contrast, the dogs often anticipate the checkpoint *well before* I see the light. They show it by a sudden quickening of pace, an arousal of that incredible latent energy, the same energy that charges to the fore when they give chase to a moose, or a porcupine, the same that now carries me fast into Eagle Island.

Protection of Face and Flesh

Backward, Face!

Chapter Thirty-Six
MY WATERLOO

Ralph Connaster is king of his Eagle Island kingdom, but he reigns over no human subjects as seemingly the sole year-round resident along the 150 lonely miles from Grayling to Kaltag. Ralph provides his place for the race, and we are so appreciative of his hospitality, our only indoor R&R in the loneliness. Licking our wounds at his table, we campers are startled when someone dashes in and shouts, "Swenson won! Just heard it on the radio. Swenson won!" I look around and perceive a collective "Who cares?" Swenson, his second victory, The Iditarod Trail Committee. It's all so far away, so irrelevant to our struggle for another long week.

"Swenson Won!"

Eagle Island, my Waterloo, more than any other single spot in the entire Iditarod. What the glacier's environs are to my body, Eagle Island is to my spirit, and not just once but multiple times. Over the years, minor discouragements like the news relating to Swenson grow into full-fledged fiascos. Even as the exact location of the checkpoint shifts up and down the river, its exasperating essence persists, haunting me, piercing to my innermost self, and it's all about the dogs. If your dogs are doing well, eating and drinking eagerly, maintaining their energy and their desire, you can take almost anything. If your dogs are going south, then even the slightest additional difficulty can push you over the edge. And so it goes for me at Eagle Island — south. On four different years I will get there with my pooches and me needing a rest, but that's par for the course. On each of these four years, however, with rest over we try to leave, and fail. We head out onto the river to meet a musher's mutiny, the dogs all stopping and glaring at me as if to say, "You've got to be kidding." Then I walk with them, and I talk with them, and I tell them this is the way (to Nome) — all to no avail. After an hour, two hours, I can see that the only way they are willing to mush is back to their warm beds in the checkpoint. It's a poor command decision, but I make it, or is it made for me? Back to Eagle Island, where on two of these dismal occasions I require another twenty-four hours before convincing my mutts to leave. Once, in the midst of the mutiny, we turn around and head toward the check point, fast, since those mutts know they are returning to their beds. Needing an alternative in the worst way, I seize upon an unlikely idea. I turn the team again, and then again, and again and again. In the darkness and out on that big river and all, I have trouble keeping oriented and hope the same for the dogs. They get so confused they don't know forward from backward and just keep on running, wherever.

Another time, I might make good on my escape from Eagle, but with warm, rainy weather, the trail is very soft. It's the year of my ankle injury, and try as I might, painfully sinking into the snow as I attempt to walk in front of the leaders, I am forced to give up; and my furry friends are again happy to return, victoriously, to those warm beds.

And yet another time, I arrive at Eagle not with a broken ankle but a broken runner. The checker, Jim Gallea, points out that the other one is coming apart too. Now, whereas managing a sled with a broken runner is one-legged tedium, two broken runners is a no-legged impossibility, I think. A lengthy bilateral restoration ensues, also another delay.

My day most disastrous at The Island I have saved for last. It will be in 2007, the year of the deep snow—ten feet on the level. The checkpoint is situated on a narrow slough, and my team has been resting high on one bank, with facilities high on the opposite bank. Those facilities include a portable outhouse, this time not quite portable enough. Yes indeed, as I'm bootying my critters for departure, wading in snow up to waist-deep, nature issues her most strident call. Having bootied at least one dog too many, I take off, wallowing mightily in full trail regalia, down my side of the slough, along the slough itself, up the other side, and then clinging to hope as I grope for the outhouse door. Inside, clawing at my clothes—belt buckle, Velcro, snaps, zipper—I damn near pull it off, but instead make half of my semi-liquid deposit while still standing in the outhouse bank. Not good. Ordinarily a few swipes of Iditarod's finest T.P. would suffice to clean up such a mess—all over the seat, on the floor, in my drawers. But at -30 F it's no use, and it instantly ices over like a hockey rink. There's no help for it, and I open the door for the female musher next in line and pray we will both get through this. Surely she will remember, and I apologize no end, as you might say. I also apologize to anyone remotely in my vicinity the next two days until, most awkward, I reach a change of underwear in Unalakleet.

Chapter Thirty-Seven
FUNNELED

So, unacquainted with future parting perils associated with Eagle Island, I make ready for my departure, along with that of the Executive Camping Party. Without specific discussion of the matter, we now feel committed to Nome or bust, and to that end together. The wind undiminished, it has intensified, and it sires an ominous portent. It is late afternoon by the time we get moving, almost two hours in Gene's wake, and sundown ushers in another long night on the Yukon. About two hours later we round a long, sweeping turn from right to left, which heads us into the teeth of the tempest, and unknowingly into a locally infamous wind funnel. I stumble upon the other teams, abruptly in the blowing, blinding snow, when my leaders bump up against a musher's behind. "That you, Ron?!" I shriek rhetorically, with not even a rhetorical response. No one hears me over the wind's howl, but I shriek again as I draw near to the musher, whom I've taken to be Gould. I discover it's Don Montgomery who moans, "Uh…I can't make any headway into the wind. Ron and Harry are stopped too. There, in front of me… You think your team will go?" "We'll see. So far I'm doing okay, but then I've been tailing you guys (my team helped out by the fresh scent of your dogs)…I'll try." I get my team around the others, and we're able to move ahead, led by Foxie and still without Gene, only assuming he's somewhere in front. No need to assume very long—about twenty minutes—and there he is, hunkered down like the others. I communicate something to him, along the lines of, "This is a real bitch, huh Gene?" Gene nods. "See if you can follow me." We creep on, like a man walking. Wind impinges upon the sled, upon me and upon the dogs, almost terminating our forward progress. Foxie and her teammates give it all they've got, heads down, bodies just above the river ice, straining forward in their harnesses; and I love to watch them, in both awe and gratitude as with each step they show how our best friend wants so badly to please us. Even such a strong bond has a limit, and we reach it after less than another mile. As related at the very beginning of this narration, this is where I am in front of the dogs, rope-tethered to Foxie, on my knees with knifed hand stabbing the ice and inching forward — but finally giving up and lying motionless.

Foxie Again. He Earned It.

I'm not sure what my next move will be, or when, but then Ron is enjoining me with, "Jim, get up. We're all here, all five of us. Got to go back and try to find a fish camp." Earlier, before dark, I took in a few small cabins on the hillside above the river, and that is our intended destination now, as we hope we can spot them in the storm and at night. Retracing obliterated tracks, we're able to move, downwind. In less than an hour we come close to the river's west bank, close enough to one of the buildings. Off the river and up the hillside we go until gaining the elevation of the fish camp cabin, out of the wind amid the (heavenly) trees. After caring for and rewarding our canines, we go inside. The cabin isn't much, just four plasticized walls, a patchwork roof and a dirt floor, but with some logs ablaze in the small woodstove it is surely God-sent, and in no time we're falling asleep, grateful as we contemplate how we could still be out on the wind-scoured Yukon.

Contemplation

Over the years I will travel this part of the Yukon River many more times. More than half of those times I will face into the wind, but only one more time into as ferocious a wind as in '79. That will be in 2009, the year dubbed *Nature's Fury* in an *Iditarod Insider* DVD when the whole field gets hammered for two interminable days by an arctic hurricane, forcing some teams to turn around and run for their lives to the prior checkpoint—or to camp in exposed circumstances. Early on I try to leave Grayling but, along with Ryan Redington, am temporarily turned back by the wind and deep snowdrifts. By late the next day, the hurricane unabated, I have exited Eagle Island into that same left turn and the "funnel" when nature brings her hammer down and nearly stops me dead in my tracks. Struggling forward, I come upon musher Bill Cotter, digging into his sled. Cotter indicates he'll be moving momentarily and is swallowed up by the swirling snow as I pass by. A short while later I'm together with another team, that driven by one Harry Alexie, an Alaskan Native from the lower Kuskokwim region who is driving a team owned by Lance Mackey. I lead, and the others follow as we fight our way upriver through the ground blizzard. It's not much fun and a little scary, but I take some comfort from knowing that with me are Cotter, a grizzled veteran of the mushing wars, and Alexie, a young Yupik Eskimo who grew up on such a river and has no doubt endured even more severe conditions. Coming upon two more teams at a partially sheltered river bend, I pull off the beaten path and stop, knowing that bend as the only relative haven on the long run to Kaltag. Alexie pulls in with me, and we both feed our dogs. He walks over and sits down, offering me some food. We munch a bunch, at first in silence. Then he speaks—at once grateful, modest, complimentary, surprising, and unnerving. "Mr. Lanier, I thank you for being here. I didn't think I was going to make it back there." So there you have it. I'm now more than a *little* scared as I comprehend the shaky nature of our mutual reliance. Sometimes it's better not to know.

Chapter Thirty-Eight
CRIPPLED

At sunrise we awake in that God-sent cabin to a break in the weather—cold but calm, or at least calmer. Just cold, meaning the absolute temperature, even down to 30 or 40 below, is tolerable without wind. Wind is what can create a difficult situation, as can be discerned from events in the preceding chapter. Therefore, our bodies rejuvenated and our spirits lifted (even including Ron's), with some degree of enthusiasm we now repack our sleds, hitch up our dogs, and descend to the river. Any obvious trail has been blown away, but with unlimited visibility we can see a few remaining markers (as well as signs posted by schoolchildren), and we handle the five or six hours to Kaltag in routine fashion, whatever that is.

Kaltag Artwork

Oh Boy, Almost There!

Before checking in at Kaltag, it is time to backtrack to *Ophir and Beyond*. Why? Because there's tales to tell, and because the Northern Route, the route not taken in 1979, is too rich in Iditarod history, both the race and otherwise, to ignore. Apropos of that history, many of the present-day race trails were utilized long ago by sourdough sled dog teams during gold rush days, and by Alaska Native peoples since antiquity. All of that, plus the genesis and the running of the first Last Great Race are capably chronicled in other works, for example Rod Perry's *Trail Breakers, Pioneering Alaska's Iditarod, Volumes I and II*. Such is not my subject, so I will not attempt further comment here. What I *will* do, and cannot ignore, is relate some of the most notable occurrences over the course of my many excursions through the northern mid-portion of the race.

Let's begin with the first time I travel the Northern Route, in 1984. It's the year of the water, of the wetness in the Rainy Pass to Farewell region, and of official congratulations for "Swimming to Nome." Swim to Nome I do not because by Nikolai, and afterward, the weather turns cold, down to minus 25. The wetness, however, sloshes on in the form of not yet frozen overflow on the Innoko River, a river B*eyond Ophir*. Unfortunately, the trail at several points crosses the river and at other times is routed upon it, so I must cope with water up to a foot deep, resulting in well-watered boots and cold feet, and setting me up for the amputation many years hence. For all that, my real trial comes after the sloshing. Attempting to gain Cripple, the next checkpoint nearly 80 miles past Ophir, I mush on and on, doggedly, well past midnight to about 2 AM but do not reach it. I was informed that the checkpoint is a mile or so off the main trail, and that a left turn is required to avoid passing by and missing Cripple altogether. At one point I hear howling from off to my left, which I take for a pack of wolves. An hour passes, two hours. Could that wolf pack have been dogs in the checkpoint? Finally I convince myself that I must have missed the turn and am now on my way to Ruby, another 80 miles. Many moons ago Malcolm Dockerty, a Mayo Clinic professor and a poet (and my pathology instructor), took delight in musing, "A man convinced beyond his will, remains a bull-headed bastard still." Bull-headed and bastardly, I now turn around and head back toward Ophir for about three hours, until concluding that I have made a huge mistake, that I had not missed the turn, that wolves were not dogs, and that the dogs all need a rest.

Lacking straw, I dress them in their cold weather coats, feed them the last of my dog food, and then watch with a certain envy as they nestle into the soft snow. All I have for me is a frozen candy bar that thaws reluctantly in my mouth, after I wrench off pieces of it with my molars. It's washed down with the last of my Capri Suns, carried warm and watery in a deep pocket next to my skin. That snack is woefully short on nutrition and hydration, but it must suffice. Then comes my turn to nestle. The site most comfortable and most conducive to a restful snooze would be in my sleeping bag, inside the sled bag, without outer clothes and boots. Trouble is, it might be *too* conducive, too likely to lead to sleep beyond the hour, two hours at most, prescribed for efficient racing. So here's what I do, and what I usually do: My sled made as soft and hammock-like as possible and my body dressed in all my warm clothes, lying supine on the hammock, face up, mitted hands hanging at sled-side, booted feet on the snow, I sleep like the dead. This technique works well when the temperature is well below zero, because after about an hour the cold wakes me, cruelly but more dependably than any alarm clock. Each time my waking thought is, "My God, I'm freezing to death!" It propels me up off the sled, onto my feet, and into five minutes of calisthenics that would impress a Marine drill sergeant. Realizing I might not die after all, I continue warming up by breaking camp, and we resume moving down the trail. In this case it means on to Cripple, that elusive left turn coming only a mile past where I turned around. Damn!

Like Eagle Island, Cripple is another checkpoint that over the years will undergo changes in venue but, again like Eagle Island, not in name or gravity. And like the Cripple of 1984, finding it will ironically require a left turn off the otherwise straight-ahead trail and throw a monkey wrench into the best laid plans of more than one aspirant to higher Iditarod office. A prime example is John Baker, in 2010. John will be in the chase, ruminating on how it might be his turn to stand in the winner's circle, when he gets disoriented, becomes convinced he bypassed Cripple and spends several frustrating, wasted, lost hours endeavoring to find it—and himself. (Sounds a lot like my missed turn in '84.) Any chance of race victory is lost too. It prompts him to state, resolutely and later in Nome, that he will never race again, without a GPS. And would you believe it, the very next year race rules are amended to permit the use of a GPS for the first time. (It will also permit John to win, apparently.) Note: John Baker cultivates respect in children, and he requests, even *insists,* that my son Jimmy call him "Mr. Baker." On the day after John's victory in 2011 thirteen-year-old Jimmy will send "Mr. Baker" a congratulatory email, from "Mr. Lanier."

The worst, and also most bizarre, case of confusion at Cripple of which I have secondhand knowledge will crop up in 2004, and to none other than my wife, Anna. Anna and I are both in the race, and I was asked, prior to race start, if I had a goal, such as top ten. My answer, my goal, was "To beat my wife," which I took to be a cinch since I would be driving our "A" team, and Anna the "B." You can imagine my chagrin when, by Nikolai, she is leading me by several hours and not so very far out of first place. Let me tell you, chagrin can be a powerful motivator because by Ophir I'm hard on her heels. For the next several hours, *Beyond Ophir* and on our way to Cripple, the two of us trade the lead back and forth in a spousal game of cat and moose. Arriving at Cripple, I have not seen Anna for some time but expect she is not far behind. She does not appear, however, not for six more hours. Other mushers show up, reporting Anna as camped short of the checkpoint. Anna's story, told much later, is this: A few hours *Beyond Ophir*, she was drifting off and took one of the Vivarin tablets I had given her (heh, heh, heh) to ward off sleep. Then things blurred a bit, and she took another Vivarin, or two or six. Meanwhile, one hour lapsed into two, three, and still no Cripple. Hills, long and languid, rolled endlessly before her while Cripple played its mind game, as the top competitors play mind games on each other. Anna, persuaded she must have nodded her way past the checkpoint, stopped inattentively, right on the trail. She fed her dogs the last of her depleted food supply and waited for what was taking shape in the cobwebs of her mind. One musher, Norwegian Kjetil Backen, went by and then another, probably guessing Anna was into some hard-to-figure stratagem. Finally, hours after she had stopped, a Good Samaritan came along on a snowmachine and pulled over to see if Anna was safe and sound. Satisfied to the contrary, he provided her with some brownies and a hot drink, and she explained her situation. She said she was perfectly fine, that she was in a movie, that she would push the fast-forward button and be transported, effortlessly and electronically, to the checkpoint. She asked, "Are you in my movie too?" It being obvious that Anna's hallucination was not going to fast-forward her anywhere, the Samaritan encouraged her to push her dogs' buttons, which she did and pulled in to Cripple just twenty minutes later.

Chapter Thirty-Nine
NORMAN

Cripple to Ruby is long enough—nine to ten hours—and hilly enough, and remote enough. It can be cold enough, but it will always be astonishingly uncomplicated for me. Its second half courses a veritable highway, on the face of it a road to nowhere, although I might conjecture that it serves some high purpose, like the transport of gold or other mined material. After about three hours on that road one reaches the broad valley of the aforementioned Yukon River, that fabled freeway of the North, waterway in summer and ice road in winter. Early in the twentieth century the Yukon was the supply route for gold-mining districts from Dawson to Fairbanks to Nome, and to Iditarod. In 1925 it became an overnight sensation when it served as the route for the diphtheria serum carried by the sled dog teams in the world-renowned serum run, from Nenana to Nome. Following a 1995 serum run led by Joe Redington, Sr., in 1997 the venerable Norman Vaughan, ninety-two years young, will lead the first of his *Serum 25* expeditions—by dog team and by snowmachine—to commemorate the 1925 original. Anna and I are members of that serum run reembodiment, and we were instrumental in its organization, even in its title. Our son Jimmy accompanies, Anna being seven months pregnant. As in 1925, *Serum 25* starts in Nenana, with Norman receiving a vial of antitoxin (and swearing that it's the real thing) from an Alaska Railroad train, and then proceeds down the Nenana River to the Tanana, then to the Yukon. I drive a dog team and Anna a snowmachine, for the most part. About the third night Anna and I, with Norman, are the last to reach the day's destination—a very old, rotting, condemnable hovel of a cabin, overflowing with the grimy, snoring bodies of our companions. Unfazed and backed up by his wife Carolyn, Norman erects a tent and crawls in for the night. Anna and I, tentless and Anna weeping, flop down artlessly on a tarp, a flap of which we roll over us while snow, alternating with a fine rain, falls silently. Comes dawn, fitful sleep giving way to the startled realization that we are overlaid by half a foot of the snow; comes Jerry Riley, expedition guide and trailblazer, stripping away both tarp and snow, exposing our sad, soggy selves to his sardonic laughter; and comes the next long day down the Yukon, all the way to Ruby, foregoing another cabin to attain civilization and the optimal drying of our gear.

At Ruby *Serum 25* joins Iditarod's Northern Route, both continuing down the Yukon thereafter. When nearing Ruby in future even-year Iditarods, descending from the hills down to the river, I will ruminate fondly upon that time with Norman, Carolyn, Riley, Anna (and Jimmy) and the others, symbolically rejoining them in my memory's reincarnation of our serum run together. Some of the memories are more memorable than others. An example is our reception in Galena, the next stop past Ruby. It is the scene of a much ballyhooed potlatch (a gathering for the celebration of practically anything), which for this potlatch includes our trip to Nome. In attendance is Edgar Nollner, the only 1925 serum musher still alive, and I have the privilege of meeting him. Also on hand, flown in from Anchorage, is Mary Lou Whitney, an heiress from New York who, like many others, has taken a cotton to Norman and coughed up some sponsorship funds for *Serum 25*'s inaugural run.

Days later we pull in to Unalakleet, and after a long day we're all tired. In a school gymnasium I'm looking for Norman, and in a far corner lies his body, on the floor. Poor old guy, plum tuckered out. On closer inspection I realize it is Carolyn, approximately thirty-five years younger than the colonel and, giving her due doubt benefit, nursing a cold. Inquiring into Norman's whereabouts, I'm told he was last seen roaring around town on his snowmachine, trying to locate some woman.

One more thing about Norman. He's no spring ptarmigan, but his mind is sharp for ninety-two, and his spirit soars like the proverbial hawk. At one point, that spirit will soar his snowmachine over an embankment, where it dives into deep snow and sinks in, stuck. In only minutes, I happen upon him. How to extract his machine, and Norman, is a no-brainer: Simply attach the machine's front end to my dog team and pull. Deferring to his status as our leader, I let Norman verbalize the plan, and then I tie off to his snowmachine. One good yank suffices to get him moving, so score one for old-fashioned pooch power.

If my deference implies condescension, such is not the case, I can assure you. Not just the titular head of our little band of dog mushers and snowmachiners, Norman is *in command*, or could be whenever needed, as events will prove. About a week out of Nenana, the trail's rigors wear thin on some of the participants. Bickering factions erupt, threatening an Eagle Island-sized mutiny and the dissolution of *Serum 25*. Norman, forever the consummate and most affable gentleman, respectfully calls a meeting, about number eleven. (He must have *liked* to call meetings, since he called at least one every day.) Wisely, without addressing the petty differences directly, he speaks as in parables, rising above the trifling fray of the day and demonstrating to all that a larger purpose is at hand, that being the good of the expedition and our shared humanity. This mastery of the mutinous moment will happen more than once. Let there be no mistake about it. Norman Vaughan, God rest his soul, was a real leader.

Jim, Norman and Anna (and Jimmy) at the Finish of Serum 25

Chapter Forty
NORTHERN WHITES

The Yukon River portion of the race's Northern Route, from Ruby to Galena to Nulato to Kaltag, is kinder than the Yukon portion of the Southern Route. In a way, it is not *"Beyond Ophir"* because it's not so unknown or unknowable, intimidating or wild. A bit of a breather as a rule, checkpoints are closer together, the prevailing wind is more or less at your back and, important for me, there is no Eagle Island! In 2006 one of those more or less at your back winds will be raking me over, shortly after I have left Ruby and am out on the Yukon, punching my way through snowdrifts. A guy on a snowmachine motors by and stops not far ahead. With my team and the situation requiring most of my attention, I don't notice the camera as I glide past him. Months later I am at work at the hospital when I'm told by Dr. Paul Steer, Zack Steer's father, that I made *Sports Illustrated*. And so there I am (or there we were) in the Dec. 25, 2006 - Jan. 1, 2007 issue — a sled dog centerfold, battling the elements and captioned *"Very Cool Runnings."* I guess so.

Cool? Very
Photo (appearing as book's cover) Courtesy of Al Grillo, grillophoto@gmail.com

I also guess it's a good time to mention the incredible views of the heavens. Dog mushing out in the country offers innumerable wondrous sights, and none more wondrous than the myriad stars on a clear, cold night, unless it's the Northern Lights on a clear, cold night. The Lights are what inspired "Northern Whites Kennel," the appellation I coined for my collection of all-white Alaskan Huskies. (See *Team Northern Whites* in photo, page 53.) Awed by the aurora's vivid colors, dancing 'cross the sky, you are oft-times satisfied to feast on that spectral spectacle for hours on end. One peek is enough to take your breath away, and breathless it will be at Nulato in 2008—an unbelievable display, the entire sky a colored canvas, the most spectacular I have ever witnessed. Spectacular, and also almost tangible, like you could reach out and touch it – yet surrealistic, eerie, even odd. Those Northern Lights have indeed seen queer sites (R. Service) but none much queerer, or dearer, than themselves.

Still in 2008, I leave Nulato after peering above one last time, and then I peer toward Kaltag, the next checkpoint at only thirty-five miles. Ahead of me is Paul Gebhardt, and ahead of Paul is Martin Buser. Every so often I can see the faint glow of their headlamps, as viewed from the rear; but then darkness again, the aurora having faded and an ice fog obliterating the stars and the faint, cold sliver of a moon. An all-encompassing curtain of night drawn down over my claustrophobic little world of team and sled, visible only in the confining beam of my headlamp, I strive to stay awake and to maintain a façade of reality. I know I'm on a river, by definition flat, but it seems aslant, from right down to left, or is it me who's aslant? My eyes probe the blackness for an orienting riverbank, a shrub, anything. But nothing's there, absolutely nothing. It must be because everything is too distant and too foggy; and I'm foggy too, even more than before the probe. Now we're going up. No, that's crazy. We're on a *river*, idiot! I blink my hoar-frosted eyelids, but I'm still going up, and not up as onto a gravel bar but as onto a long, broad hillside. Wake up, Lanier! You're losing it!...There! Yes, it's there! Paul's barely perceptible headlamp, a fleeting reference to time and space. But then, the barely perceptible extinguished, I return to my constricted, confusing unreality. A dog becomes mildly tangled. Ordinarily I would keep moving, awaiting self-resolution of the tangle. Now, however, glad for an excuse to stop, I do so and walk up to the dog. By then the tangle is no more, and I return to the sled. That little walk, all fifty feet of it, serves to elevate my consciousness and confirm that the river is undeniably flat. Fleetingly assured and back on the sled, I am soon on the foggy hillside again, my walk a waste of time in two ways. This maddening state of affairs hangs on for the next three hours and like forever, but finally we *do* ascend a small rise and pass by some willows on an island. Such claustrophobic confusion is rampant on the inky-dark, featureless nighttime landscape of the rivers, the ocean, or even a swamp. The madness stalks me until I see streetlights and mush up onto a street where as in 1979, I check in at Kaltag.

Chapter Forty-One
ANOTHER GOOD SAMARITAN

At Kaltag I've gone full circle, the left 180 degrees the Southern Route, the right the Northern. I do this not in the same race of course, but in this book's fantasy Iditarod, a grand and happily romanticized version—all quite *Beyond Ophir*. Now as to Kaltag itself, if the wind is blowing down the river, it is blowing in the unprotected and undesirable spot where your team is sleeping, or trying to sleep, and some years that is the case. Also, in spite of efforts to ensure safety, snowmachines can speed by, alarmingly close. I don't know if any injuries have ever occurred, hopefully not. (Of course, Kaltag is not the only place where snowmachines and dog teams may not coexist so well, especially when alcohol fuels the snowmachiner.) An option is to press on past the checkpoint, ideally to the idyllic but easily missed "Tripod" cabin at somewhere near twenty-five miles. On Southern Route years this is too far, by and large, because you've already made the long run from E. Island. Anyway, in 1979 Kaltag it is for the next several hours.

During those hours I have occasion to converse with Rich Burnam, veteran musher and checker. I first met Rich in 1978, in McGrath and Unalakleet when doing the psychometric testing on the mushers, and one thing stood out. He wore glasses, thick ones, and they were repeatedly frosting over, necessitating frequent *de*frosting with a finger or otherwise mushing blind, which at times must have been the case. I've got to hand it to him for making it to Nome, and he did it well enough. I know what I'm talking about here because in my first race I am myopic too. Contact lenses help me a lot, though they become uncomfortable after a few days without extraction from my eyeballs. In a few years I will benefit from having my corneas lasered.

After those hours and having departed Kaltag, the next twenty miles are protracted ones due to a compilation of lots of soft snow, lots of moguls (snowy undulations caused by snowmachines), and lots of steady climbing up into the Nulato Hills. In 1979 the pace is discouraging but mitigated by the unanticipated and stunning scenery with snow-capped hills and foliage. Over the years, however, I will become less impressed by the scenery and more impressed, actually *de*pressed, by the pokey pace. An hour into this portion of the race, I'm often afraid I might not ever get through it, and one time I won't—almost.

The Scenery...

...and More of It...

…and More

In the 1984 race, the "Swimmer," I will leave Kaltag in a warm snowfall with rapidly accumulating, moist, heavy snow. I climb even more protractedly than usual and feel more depressed than usual with the onset of weakness and nausea. After about two hours the nausea leads to its conclusion, wrenching me to a halt. Having pulled my team off the trail and thrown each team member a snack, I collapse carelessly into my sled and remain collapsed there for several hours. Alternating between barfing and shivering as the wet snow piles up, I get weaker as my bag gets wetter. Two mushers go by without so much as a "howdy do," perhaps taking me for an intentional camper. But then along comes *my* Good Samaritan, a musher named Fred Agree, who sees I'm in need and judges that I could be in danger. He claims he's had practice caring for mountain climbers incapacitated by cold exposure and that my damp, debilitating condition might have me headed that way. So he offers some hot coffee and bagels, the bagels given him by his mother back in some big city in the Lower Forty-Eight, and then he covers the top of my sled bag so as to impede the flow from the melting snow. The coffee and bagels come right back up, but the thought was there. Observing that my illness (food poisoning?) refuses to let up, Fred turns his team around and returns to Kaltag to summon help, a noble gesture for sure since it sets his race back as much as a whole half day.

Going on four hours later, the help arrives in the form of two gents on snowmachines, an Alaska State trooper and Old Four Eyes, Rich Burnam. They have come to evacuate me (or my body) back to Kaltag. By that time, incongruously, I'm feeling a tad better, and when two more dog teams come along, I suggest I might muddle through if they will only lead the way. So off I go, my condition improving by the minute, all the seventy miles to Unalakleet. I will not see Agree again until Nome where I not only thank him personally (and publicly at a mushers' banquet) but also apologize for my continuing on down the trail after his sacrifice, explaining that I had not planned my illness, nor my recovery. Taking it all in stride, he tells me that no apology is needed, that he much prefers my recovery to the alternative, and I *Agree* with that (pun intended).

The whole Samaritan incident reminds me of the fine miseries. Iditarod is loaded with them, also with the not so fine, and then some miseries that are just, well, miserable. Like vomiting on the trail, one of my favorites. Fact is, at some stage in each of my Iditarod races there will be at least one time when I am so low, so tired, so sick, so sleepy, so thirsty, so lost, so disoriented, so disheartened, so behind, so wet, so cold, so frostbitten, so concerned about my dogs or so damned disgusted that I try not to think about it. Much is repressed, or I can fool myself into believing that next time will be different. Of course I know it's doing that same thing that same way and expecting something other than that same result. Not bloody likely.

Chapter Forty-Two
AN OLD WOMAN

The Executive Camping Party starts out for Unalakleet, at ninety miles one of the longest runs in the Iditarod. All through its first half, as mentioned in the prior chapter, I am much taken with the gorgeous, undulating and verdant landscape, out of the blue because I expected a color-poor, dull plane with very few trees, based on my memory of previous visits to the arctic/subarctic communities of Nome, Kotzebue, and also Unalakleet. Weather is a factor, the morning's calm under a cloudless, sunny sky being long sought during the prior two days and nights on the cold, dark, wind-scoured Yukon. Anyhow, speaking for myself, I move along contentedly, and by midafternoon we are holed up at Old Woman, over halfway to Unalakleet. Not just a cabin, Old Woman is also a locality, and it features a strikingly stark mountain of the same name. Local legend has it that the place is haunted by an Eskimo woman, long ago old, before she was dead. The 1979 cabin, in disrepair and bypassed in future races, will be updated by a nice, new Bureau of Land Management replacement. Nevertheless, the otherworldly aura of that aged, even ancient woman will live on. When I take five there, about five hours in 1979, I am all the while alert to her presence. She is in some ways more sobering than scary, and being there is like paying homage to a respected elder, if you assume the respected part. On the few occasions when I bypass the old woman I regret it, feeling I have made a strategic error by prolonging my run all the way to Unalakleet, another thirty-six miles. The error is not only strategic, surely, it is also spiritual, disrespectful of the specter, cultivating her disapproval and deserving of her wrath. I know of more than one musher who will tempt fate, spurn the old woman's blessing, overextend his or her dogs that extra thirty-six miles, and later pay the price when she extracts a scratch or a lengthy delay due to another mutiny.

The happening most daunting with her haunting will come in 2010 when, not heeding her call, I mush boldly on by, even though my team is tired. After just a hundred yards it feels like a mistake, my forward motion impeded by a trail recently chewed up by snowmachines (or by a spook?); and after less than a mile I turn around and am drawn back, as if pulled by a magnet. Someone should post a sign: "Beware Old Woman—or Not, at Your Peril!"

Don Montgomery, Paying His Respects to the Old Woman?

After giving The Woman her due and Gene his head start, Harry, Don, Ron and I leave Old Woman and head for Unalakleet and "The Coast," the coast of the Bering Sea. That thirty-six miles is finally flat in the main, although overall downhill and, except for the land bordering creeks, treeless tundra. Mushing west toward the setting sun, the weather fair and calm, imparted is what could be a sense of peace and well-being, if not for a nagging discomfort at my rear, in fact *in* my rear. In the distant future sleds will be constructed with rear seats, "sit down sleds" or "tail draggers." They will take a load off and alleviate my discomfort, but not yet, not in 1979. No sir, I've now got the real deal, the logical result of riding the runners hour after hour, day after day. Not a well-known nor often reported mushing malady, but a malady to be sure. Hemorrhoids! Itching, burning, wedging, intermittently bleeding hemorrhoids — hundreds of miles of them! I don't know how many others are afflicted with this complication, it being rather easily hidden from public view, but for me it's a genuine occupational hazard and a real pain in the ass! Mine always mild in terms of the bleeding part, I do know that one other musher, author Gary Paulsen of *Winterdance* fame, will have hemorrhoidal hemorrhaging not mild at all. He will be obliged to scratch and be air evacuated when he fills his boots with blood and nearly bleeds out at a checkpoint. I will count my blessings and settle for the mere discomfort.

Shortly after the sun sets, along one of the few wooded areas, my dogs suddenly pick up their pace and appear nervous, bodies tensed and ears flattened with eyes darting furtively and in unison, first to one side and then the other. I'm sure I appear nervous too, and I cast sideways glances off into the trees but see nothing. I see nothing and I hear nothing, except the engine of an airplane overhead as it buzzes me once, then twice, before flying off into the sunset.

Many hours later, after our arrival in Unalakleet and at our hosts' home, I will phone my parents in Fargo, North Dakota. We talk about the race in general and about my race and trail travails in particular. I tell them I was just asked by a pilot if I saw the wolves, that he flew over me as a pack was close, and that I replied I had not seen them but was not surprised since my team had appeared frightened. Then my mother wants to know what I'm intending to do about it, about the wolves waiting for her son at the city limits. This takes me unawares, but I tell her I will continue on to Nome, of course, leaving Unalakleet in two or three hours, also that I love her, and I say goodbye. The point of all this is what she says next, after hanging up, to my father (and as related to me weeks later). "Oh Billy, our life is such a mess. First one daughter gets divorced, then the other marries a black man, and now our only son is in Alaska, being chased by a pack of wolves!" A word or two of explanation, even apology, might be called for here. My parents are not racists. They got over the divorce, and after an initial "Guess who's coming for dinner" reaction, they unconditionally accepted and came to love my sister's black husband, Mac. Me too. Wolves, though, that was too much!

Chapter Forty-Three
THE DORATIDI

By late evening my four companions and I are in Unalakleet. We do dog care, equipment care, people care, and then grab some shut eye before departing early the next morning. This genteel schedule of travel by day, rest by night has been enjoyed for a couple of days, not really by design. In Unalakleet, as in other checkpoints, we experience some glitches in communication since we are scattered around, some distance apart and often without telephones (or cell phones, iPhones, iPads, laptops, etc.). This stumbling block surmounted, we ascertain that everyone is okay or not, and that poor old Gene Leonard will try to leave by such and such a time. Then the rest of us make our plans.

The Town of Unalakleet from a Roof Top

A Kennel on the Coast of the Bering Sea, Self-Flushing with the High Tide

The Young and the Old

Getting out of town in the predawn darkness proves difficult. It begins on an icy river, after which comes bare ground and more ice, leading up onto a gravely road, and then you're whipped down into a ditch and through an alder patch, all with only an infrequent marker to show the way. Lots of rookies get lost here, and I am no exception. Finally I hit upon a better defined path, still with ice and gravel as well as overflow, but now I'm on some likeness of a trail, hopefully the one to Nome. Then comes a series of hills, the "Blueberry Hills" (as in Fats Domino). With Ron nearby and the others not, we work our way up those hills, often off the sled and jogging along as much and as fast as our athleticism allows. Despite the doffing of a layer or two, this results in sweat-soaked clothing, the negative effects of which will come later. But now, almost at the climb's culmination, I slip past some small, gnarled trees that in a future year will be the site of a wreck. It's when Anna and I fly to Nome, synchronous with the start of the Iditarod in Anchorage, to commence the Doratidi, i.e. "Iditarod" backwards. The idea is to mush from Nome to Anchorage, or as far as time away from work, as well as dog food, dog power, will power and numerous other imponderables will allow. We know we will be running head-on into the Iditarod, but that's not the wreck I have in mind.

Incidentally (and digressingly), the word "wreck" has a certain singular significance in mushing circles, if you've been around the game as long as I have. Back in the day, during the Anchorage Fur Rendezvous Sled Dog Race, an irrepressible old Fin by the name of Orville Lake held forth on local radio and TV, commenting on the race from beginning to end. (Orville did the same from checkpoint to checkpoint throughout the first Iditarod, in 1973.) He was fond of using the "wreck" word in reference to any mismush, and with relish to one that caused delay and might result in a win for another musher. Orville may not have coined the term, but he used it effectively.

My wreck, or more specifically *Anna's*, will occur during the Doratidi as we traverse those hills, backwards, towards Unalakleet. Each of us is running a team, Anna's well ahead of mine as we near the gnarled trees. I'm impressed by the extent to which they have been violated, as if struck by a missile, say a loaded sled at full downhill speed. Not long afterward I come to an open, level tract, and there's Anna, her team and her sled, or what's left of it. The sled is half its pre-wreck height, not broken down as for shipment in a small plane but just broken — the brush bow, the handle bar and two stanchions all in pieces. Anna is broken too, or at least very discouraged. I do my best to pick up her spirits and then start picking up sled parts, but things are way beyond repair. So I lash Anna's sled to my sled and tie our teams together as one unit, about twenty-five dogs long.

Then, with Anna as my passenger, we are moving again. Overloaded and imbalanced, and with too much dog power, it's no walk in the park, but we get by. Long past midnight we come to a seaside area, near Egavik, a former reindeer herding station on the Bering seacoast. We notice some large tracks in the snow, fresh and not like those of a moose or caribou. Anna and I are so on task that we don't stop to investigate. The dogs don't stop either, but they act like they've seen a wolf, or a ghost. In front of us and far off the trail I see a pair of small, beady eyes, moving to the left, and then another pair of eyes, moving to the right. *We* move *forward* and "drop kick me Jesus through the goalposts," right between those eyes and past them, wondering what has just happened.

An hour later we hit the outskirts of Unalakleet, that icy, gravelly north side of it, and make our way to our grand entrance, but nobody's there. After all, it's 6 AM. I fasten down the team and walk up to what happens to be Brown's Restaurant. To my astonishment, a man opens the door and yells "Dog team! The first dog team is here!" He mistakes me for the leader of the Iditarod, even though that leader is not expected until later that morning. But what the heck, for a few moments Anna and I are leading the race! Such a letdown all around when our unintentional imposturing is unmasked. We then get down to brass tacks and ask where we can tether our dogs, and ourselves. It eventuates that Doug Kachetag, the checker and one day Iditarod Hall of Famer, will serve as our host. With time running out, our Doratidi must terminate in Unalakleet, although I hang around a few more days. I drive a team to Old Woman and back before loading the dogs and our equipment, and me, on an Alaska Airlines jet bound for Anchorage. Anna flies home earlier, but not before we spend some time on the town.

Doug's father, Fred Kachetag, invites us to his home for breakfast. Fred serves up some great pancakes and then tells us an even greater story. As a young man, probably in the 1920's, he and his dog team ventured far to the east, past Old Woman, and encroached upon Indian Territory. Suddenly and at close range, he bumped into another young man, an Athabaskan Indian from Kaltag. For centuries, the Eskimo and the Indian had been enemies, sometimes to the death, and the animosity and distrust persisted. Very cautiously, these two men eyed each other, sat down a short ways apart, and managed to communicate about trapping, the weather, whatever. Fred said that the entire time he kept his finger on the trigger of his rifle, hidden under a blanket. Many years later, after a thaw in the political climate, the two of them met again, worked together as members of an Alaska Native organization, and became friends. They shared joint memories of that first meeting, taking into account how both of them had employed the blanketed trigger finger.

After the breakfast we're lounging around and hear that musher Jerry Austin reported seeing two polar bears, in close proximity to Egavik. This completes the picture of those tracks in the snow and the small, beady eyes on left and right, too far for my headlamp to reveal the white bodies. We dropped kicked thru the goalposts all right, right between two polar bears (apparently as rare as hens' teeth in the Unalakleet region)! Now knowing what happened, I relate it to Doug who grabs his rifle, a few friends and, like a vigilante posse in the Old West, rides out of Dodge on snowmachines to apprehend the brutes, unsuccessfully.

Bering Sea Sunset, Framed by a Fish Rack

Chapter Forty-Four
DANCING WITH WIND

At the summit of the Blueberries one beholds a fantastic panorama. To the right, to the east, are endless hills, filling the horizon and framing uninhabited, snowy valleys, begging to be explored. Ahead, north and west, is a breathtaking view of coastal Iditarod—Norton Bay and then the continuing coast of the Bering Sea, fading into the far distance as it reaches for Nome. Before all that, however, comes a more immediate goal, the next checkpoint of Shaktoolik. I can see it, a tiny speck miles away, at the end of a narrow spit betwixt the sea and a lagoon. Even more immediate is the ride *down* the Blueberries on a wide though precipitous trail descending hundreds of feet to sea level. Without snow it would be a real challenge, but not to worry. On some basis, topographical or meteorological or other, snow is reliably there, so mushing down Blueberry's backside is actually fun. It's so much fun that in 1979, when I reach the ride's end, execute a gee turn and head out along that narrow spit, I'm unprepared for what hits me, like a slap in the face—wind, a cold north wind. It comes out of nowhere, the entire jaunt up and over the hills having been windless. Now the negative effect of my athleticism and sweat-soaked clothing comes to bear. In a short while I don my parka and my wind suit, but too late. Nearly two long, bone-chilling hours later, I shiver down the one narrow street of Shaktoolik, itself narrow astride that spit of land. Weak with hypothermia, I force myself to perform the usual and requisite care of the critters, in the small lee of my host's abode. Any thoughts I may someday entertain about blowing through that checkpoint and heading without delay for Koyuk, fifty miles into the wind athwart Norton Bay, is now just a cruel joke.

In general, villages are located where hills and trees provide protection from the big blows of winter. Shaktoolik is an exception. I was raised in the flatness of Fargo, North Dakota, where you can stand on a beer can and see the other side of town. In Shaktoolik it's the same, but in Shaktoolik you could see the next county, if there were a next county, and there are no trees or other protection. Incessantly exposed, often to a wind of gale force, "Godforsaken" comes to mind. Why would anyone want to live there? Why was it chosen as a home site? The answer, I gather, is that the sea provides, in the form of fish, crab, seals, and so forth. In any case, the people in Shaktoolik appear thriving and happy, as much as anywhere along the Iditarod Trail. They certainly welcome us mushers and do what they can to make our stay enjoyable and recuperative. In 2010 they will also make it profitable for me when I buy a lottery ticket from a young girl. About a day later, in the Elim checkpoint, I'm notified that as the winner of the "Shaktoolik Sweepstakes" I am the proud owner of a new snowmachine helmet!

It is early evening, and with a normalized body temperature I am revitalized, if only temporarily. I've had food, drink and a catnap. It's time to go. The weather forecast, not encouraging, is for continued wind throughout the night. A cookie, a last cup of coffee, and we can procrastinate no more. Ron and I go outside. The sun is setting, the wind is howling, and it's below zero. Now not in any way genteel, but as I said, it's time to go. We prime our critters and gladly accept the aid of some villagers who lead our teams down onto the lagoon. With some reluctance on the part of the dogs, and me too, we head north for Koyuk, into the night and into the teeth of the gale.

The reluctance reflects the fact that the dogs are getting tired, that some aspects of our pilgrimage are getting old, and even that *we* are getting old, having been on the trail for three long weeks. All of us, man and beast, have aches and pains, and we could use some time off. The man discounts the adversity and lumbers on, driven by the lure of adventure, fame, glory, the *Call of the Wild* (London), "the muck called gold" (Service), his ego, his wife, and all that. But what drives the beast? You might answer, "The man," and you would be partly correct. But as any musher worth his salt will tell you, if the dogs don't want to go, they won't, at least not very far very fast. So there's something else, something in their being that motivates them to get up, stretch their tired muscles, respond to their master's "hike" and move out, again and again for now nearly eight hundred miles. Much has been made of the connection between a man and his dog, and between a musher and his dog team. Prompted by Nicolas Petit, 2011 Rookie of the

Year, I can make light of this by joking, "The connection between me and my dogs is the gangline," but I know there's a lot more.

For the first several miles we're treated to more tundra and then drop down onto the ice. Soon comes a short land portage, a small shelter cabin and Reindeer Point (or "Iguanak," in the Inupiat language), a tall promontory rising disproportionately above the otherwise uninspired plain of the barren Bay. The Point is the only blemish on the horizon for the next forty miles, all the way to Koyuk on the other side of the bay, flat except for interspersed pressure ridges. The cabin, the Point and the ridges are rapidly blotted out as the wind intensifies, driving both the stinging snow and the cold through any openings—around your face and neck, under your parka, and most telling under your mitts to your wrists, hands and fingers. Ron and I take turns leading, striving for the trail, which heads into the wind and therefore north. We give up pretending we're on *the* trail, not having seen a marker for miles. Also, we tend to avoid veering much to the left, to the west, that being the direction of purported open leads and open ocean. Hm…. A few times we move up against one of the pressure ridges as it emerges from the whiteout. Most ridges being much longer than wide, it takes less time to go over, as compared to around. So with the lead dogs we scramble the several feet to the top, drop down the far side and sink into a snowdrift. Then we scramble in reverse to hoist the loaded sled, push it over, and lose footing as it falls. We come to dread those ridges, and progress is painful. We stop to consult each other, and then recommence the quest. Ahead of us, the lights of Koyuk could serve as a guide, but not on this trip, the lights being obliterated by the blizzard. At about 5 AM those lights finally become visible, a beacon beckoning our exhausted and yet again hypothermic bodies up off the ice and into the village.

The crossing of Norton Bay, rarely easy, will prove testing, and worse in many of my Iditarods. Interminably long, it seems even longer when Koyuk's hillside lights are *not* obliterated and then can be seen from as far as thirty miles. For hours that exasperating beacon beckons, virtually unchanged, prompting your infuriated mind (and sometimes your mouth) to cry out, "When in hell will I ever get there?!" This is even worse when the route is lengthened by deviations to circumvent opens leads, on an exasperatingly serpentine course. In 2009 my agonizing will be augmented by an ice build-up on my face, on and in the interstices of a large, full-face facemask. It is the combined result of ice crystals in the air and condensation of the breath, not to mention the spittle and snot dribbling onto my beard where it freezes tightly. I get to the point where I not only can't eat or drink through the ice,

I almost can't *see*. Dead set against stopping to rectify the situation, I hang in there with grim determination and squint my way to the lights. I would say that what the Glacier's environs are to my body, and what Eagle Island is to my spirit, Norton Bay is to my *soul*.

Norton Bay and a Pressure Ridge

Those crossings, while daunting and even soul-searching, are not without their lighter side. That face mask, mentioned in the prior paragraph and given to me by Gunnar Johnson, will have *its* lighter side, the side facing outward and featuring the fluorescing face of a skeleton, as for Halloween. Before leaving Shaktoolik for the Bay, I take five to warm up and spook the folks in the checkpoint with my mask. Its maximum effect, however, I can elicit when moving past a parked team at night. My ghoulish countenance reflected by the other musher's headlamp, I scare the bejesus out of him, and he nearly leaps out of his parka. You've got to have some fun with this mushing thing, even give birth to a hallucination or two. Like on yet another crossing, alone and in another storm, I'm in need of some time out. Near Reindeer Point, I maneuver my way over to its southern side, out of the wind, and there I find two other teams. One of the mushers is a British Islander (Rick Atkinson? Roy Monk?) who greets me with something like, "I say there, chap. Care to join us for a spot of tea?"

Geared Up for the Crossing—Reindeer Point in the Far Distance

Comes 1999. I'm holed up with two others in that small shelter cabin, very small and barely sheltering. Our three teams are crammed together, cheek to jowl, on the cabin's leeward side. This is an agreeable arrangement, providing a shield from the wind plus a warm body, or two or three, to cuddle up to, and onto. You might surmise that this would lead to disagreement and to fights, but no, it's something akin to transporting a bunch of dogs in a Cessna. In the airplane the noise/vibration-subdued dogs all lie like a rug, a very placid rug, for the entire duration of the flight. Sheltered in that lee and thankful for their warm opportunity, the dogs do the same and cuddle all the more, without argument.

My companions in the cabin are Jim Gallea on his rookie year and a mystery musher, *He who shall not be named*. We're holed up for about four hours, waiting for the raging blizzard outside to abate. It does not, and we realize we're screwed and need to brave it. So we line out our teams and start off into the night, and into the blizzard—Gallea, me, and *He*. It's tough going with minimal visibility, our way obscured by drifts and markers obscured by their absence. My main leader, Sukuma, works well when snooping out a route, and soon we're in a caravan, in the order of Jim Lanier, Jim Gallea and *The Mystery*. In such circumstances an exceptional lead dog is a wonder to behold, not to mention a lifesaver if need be. How he or she finds the trail, loses it and then finds it again, and again and again, is nothing short of miraculous.

189

It appears as a combination of smell, feel and that sixth sense, that instinct beyond my poor human comprehension. Even a sixth sense can fail, and then we fall back on walking left, walking right. At first we consider turning back, but our caravanning, though slow and not for sissies, takes us past an arguable point of no return. Creeping along for hours, it is time never-ending. At intervals I stop and wait for the others, to make sure we are all safe, and sane. On one of the stops, the three of us huddled together, I shout over the wind's howling, "You guys okay?" Gallea replies, "Yeah, but I'd like to know how far it is to Koyuk." *He who shall not* volunteers, "It is…let's see…17.3 miles." Bear in mind, in 1999 a GPS is strictly forbidden. And now you know the rest of the story, and why *He shall not be named.*

Chapter Forty-Five
SINGING IN THE BLOWHOLES

I wake up in a corrugated metal Quonset hut, which I'm told is the Koyuk Armory. It is stark, with an unadorned, monotonously arching wall/ceiling and a floor, empty except for five recuperating bodies—Gene, Harry, Don, Ron, and me. Up off the floor and on my feet, I am profoundly grateful to have made it to Koyuk and to be safely off the ice and warmed, excepting the middle knuckle on my right hand. That knuckle is still cold, as well as swollen and more strange than painful. It is vaguely reminiscent of my first take on my frostbitten fingers and toe, of being no longer part of me. Only vaguely, because I am not destined for a knucklectomy, but something tells me that joint is never going to be the same; and as foretold, many years down the pike it will balloon to nearly grotesque proportion, a victim of osteoarthritis (cryogenic or "cold-induced" osteoarthritis?), yet otherwise be mostly strange.

The Party in the Armory. Top, from Left: Ron, Don, Gene.
Bottom: Harry, the Author

The cold, the knuckle, the Quonset hut and other Koyuk architecture aside, what impresses me most are the children. I step outside the armory into bright sunshine and into the company of around fifteen uniformly bright, smiling, laughing, colorfully dressed youngsters—the kids of Koyuk. They seem happy to see me, even if they're just happy to be out of school for Iditarod, their own brand of March Madness. One of them, a boy about ten, proclaims that he is my personal valet. Vacationing students often adopt an individual musher to be his or hers, but a valet? This kid is adamant that he will bring me my water, dog food, everything. Race rules or no, how impolite it would be of me to refuse. So I don't, and he does. Somewhere I have a photo of him, and of his friends.

Photo Found—My Valet

His Friends, Outside the Armory

Over the years I will meet and be housed by and valeted by so many warm, generous people that I have lost track of some of them. Let me acknowledge all of them, or all of you, right here and now; and if any of them, or you, are reading this, I would very much like to hear from them, or you. In our Dora-tidi, Anna and I will mush each day to the next burg and dally there through the ensuing night. Where and with whom is not predetermined, but after our arrival each evening at our next port of call, some gracious villager invites us into his dwelling, not to mention allowing our teams to be staked out, fed and you know what just outside. Fat chance of that in your subdivision!

In Koyuk a few individuals come to mind, like big game guide Bob Hannon, his wife Lola and their children. I come into their debt when we are their guests during the Doratidi. On most years since, Lola pays me a visit in the checkpoint after my nap, as I sip coffee to clear the cobwebs. That nap is representative of my Iditarod sleep pattern. One hour, twice out of twenty-four, except for that first night when I'm too jacked up to doze even a minute. It's no mystery why I get spaced out, even make mistrakes! That one hour, however, makes all the difference. I'm not really recovered, but I feel like it after clearing those cobwebs, and I'm ready to go.

At that same checkpoint another person merits recognition, not only in my mind but also in the minds and memories of many other once-weary mushers.

Dionne Herman, former Koyuk schoolteacher and perennial checker, will for many years greet survivors of the ice, usher them to their parking place, provide dog water and other essentials, and in conclusion guide teams out of Dodge and back onto the trail—all with a smile. Dionne is the prototypic Iditarod volunteer—enthused, helpful, tireless and selfless. Up and down the old trail, from Forth Avenue in Anchorage to Front Street in Nome, the volunteers are what make the race possible.

Other Koyuk Architecture, Old Style

Leaving Koyuk, the five teams of *The Party* all head for Elim, fifty miles distant. The route is along the seacoast, and intermittently over some gently rolling hills. Not bad, but the prevailing atmospheric pressure differentials dictate that big blows, both frequent and ferocious, mercilessly rake the land, the dog teams and the mushers, from right to left, from land to sea, and from safety to the uncertainty of untested ocean ice. I know of only one so dangerous a deviation (Beth Baker, 1994), but when you are in an active blowhole, not able to see past your leaders and your entire team being blown seaward, the possibility does cross your mind. I'll be there a few times when a blow hole is bad, but not *real* bad. *Real* bad will be defined in 1991 when Susan Butcher leads the race out of White Mountain, with only seventy-five miles to go. Running into *real* bad, she turns around, does a head-on into Rick Swenson and reportedly yells, "It's not doable, Rick!" to which Rick reportedly replies that he will advance a short way, then turn and follow her back to the village. He does advance, until short becomes long, all night long through a storm fiercer than any he has ever faced, or never wishes to face. While Rick struggles from marker to marker, the outside world has no idea if he is dead or alive (no tracker system in 1991) until he emerges from his private reality show the next day at the aptly named checkpoint of Safety, only twenty-two miles from Nome. He mushes on to claim a trophy for his record fifth Iditarod championship. Years later he will claim a different kind of trophy, also metallic, and shared with Jim Lanier. It's one of the few things, besides sled dogs and certainly not championships, that I share with Rick Swenson: a hip replacement. Mine I receive in 2011, about a year after Rick's. I don't know about his, but my orthopedic surgeon says my hip problem may well be the result of trauma incurred in the Iditarod. Rick and I also share considerable gratitude for the medical miracle, and for its permitting us to continue our mushing careers.

Koyuk Architecture, New Style—Lining the Way Out of Dodge to
The Coast Beyond, and to Nome

Midway to Elim, the Executive Party mushes through a blowhole and samples a suggestion of bad, a breeze from our right flank, but *not* so bad for a guy with an intentionally numb nose. My nose may be numb, but my brain is capable of creative thought, or so I tell myself as I mush along and cook up ways to amuse. Many mushers plug themselves into a Sony Walkman or updated equivalent to rock and roll the long, humdrum parts of the trail. It is said that Rick rocks, whereas Gary Paulsen moves more mellow with Mahler. I like to make my own music, so I sing to the hateful team thing (and it harkens with a grin) [Service]. I also sing to the moon, the wind, in the rain. The dogs do seem to like it, and I fancy they run faster…away from me? Between Koyuk and Elim, on a long flat stretch in the late 1990s, I'll be bored out of my gourd. I sing to the team, and to myself, a tune that sticks in my head: "In the jungle, the mighty jungle, the lion sleeps tonight…." It morphs into, "In the checkpoint, the Iditarod checkpoint, the sled dog sleeps tonight…. A-wim-a-way, a-wim-a-way…. oo-oo-oo (falsetto)…I-di-ta-rod, I-di-ta-rod…" (As above, I *tell* myself I'm capable.) A few days later, when comes my turn at the podium during the Nome banquet, I let 'er rip: "In the checkpoint…oo-oo-oo…." Some people are shocked, but most say they like it, including folks in communities all over the Seward Peninsula, listening to Nome's KNOM radio broadcast. At every Nome banquet thereafter I will sing a song, a song composed (or more honestly, plagiarized) on the trail. I will now take the liberty of providing the words to one of them, one that is requested from time to time. I am aware that verse number two made its debut in Chapter 14, but the song —a regular magnum opus—is presented here in its complete entirety (Thanks, Yogi). Titled *Sixteen Dogs,* it is sung to the tune of *Sixteen Tons,* in my best Tennessee Ernie Ford imitation:

Verse 1

Some people say a man is made out of mud,
A dog musher's made out of muscle and blood,
Muscle and blood, skin and bone,
A mind that's weak and a back that's strong.

CHORUS
You load sixteen dogs, and what do you get?
Another day older and deeper in debt,
Race Marshall don't cha' call me, 'cause I can't go,
I owe my soul to the local feed store.

Verse 2

I woke up one mornin' just a-barely in time,
I leaped in my truck, and I drove to the line,
Loaded sixteen dogs, said goodbye to my home,
Then I pulled the hook, and we headed for Nome.

(CHORUS)

Verse 3

If you see me comin', better step aside,
A lot of teams didn't, a lot of teams died,
One leader of iron,
The other of steel,
If the gee one don't get ya, then the haw one will.

(CHORUS)

Verse 4

Though hopin' for the most, I'm a-headin' up the coast,
Koyuk, Elim, then givin' up the ghost,
Way out of first place, don't you think it's kind 'a queer,
That already I'm talkin', "gonna WIN NEXT YEAR!?"

(CHORUS)

Music is one of the many ways, by no means least, that I look forward to, savor and yes, obsess about the Iditarod. In future years my son, Jimmy, will join me at that podium for an annual father/son duet. Thus enhanced, the tradition and the obsession live on. Both spill over into the Covenant Church next to the burled arch at the finish line. At the Sunday morning service, the same day as the race banquet, Pastor Harvey Fiskeaux invites any and all mushers to say a few words. I take that to include "sing a few words", so Anna, Jimmy and I do just that, and we're not alone. Mike Williams, the sobriety musher, customarily offers up a song too, in Yupik and self-accompanied on his guitar; and Dee Dee Jonrowe "sings" His praises as she regales in the trail's glories.

Jimmy with his Papa, and Mac—Church in Background
Photo Courtesy of Preston and Betsy McMillan, New Hope, Minnesota

Chapter Forty-Six
ELIM, GOLOVIN, AND THE
DAILY DUMP

Elim—Looking Back Toward Unalakleet and Norton Bay

The approach to Elim is scenic, nestled amongst adjoining mountains, green forest and the sea. It is entails pumping and pole pushing up a long, upscale road to its acme and from there, looking upon the magnificence of Norton Sound. Commencing at the seashore far below, snow-white sea ice alternates with azure-blue, open ocean and extends to the far horizon, taking in

Unalakleet, the Blueberry Hills, Shaktoolik and the iced-over, pressure-ridged Norton Bay. To gaze upon all that, that which you have conquered or lived through, is both exhilarating and sobering. What a high, literally and otherwise, one of the many counter-lows. It's like Ron's "Every day, a mountain."

Standing on Another Steepled Street, in Elim

Continuing on that road, it takes us far down into the village. Again farmed out to our hosts, we eventually make contact with each other and ask Gene when he is aiming to leave. Meanwhile, I detect a certain self-containment, a self-sufficiency, almost a feeling of being walled-off from the world. Shielded by the surrounding mountains, Elim's independence may fancifully be a function of the geothermal energy that heats its nearby hot springs, and that perhaps could provide its power.

My power is provided by my dogs, and the dogs' by their dog food. After that food and some relaxation, we power out of there and again onto the trail. On the ocean for several miles, Ron and I miss the exit back onto land and go well past it until acknowledging our error. Then we zigzag all over tarnation to ultimately course-correct and begin a long, taxing climb to well above the tree line (only about two hundred feet elevation at this latitude) and then to the top of "Mount McKinley," so-named by the locals.

Another spectacular vista is enjoyed only briefly before we glide down into a valley, the prelude to another climb, then another. After a few miles, this culminates as we crest a final mountaintop, the last one before a long, snowless, rough descent with challenging side-hilling, returning us to sea level on Golovin Bay. As we crest that top we are greeted by a stiff wind, perhaps from one of those blow holes. I am suddenly eager to head down, to leave the blow at my back, but just then we catch sight of a team, or the headlamp of a team, far down in a valley below and to our right, more than ninety degrees from where the trail is heading. We deduce that it's a wandering Don Montgomery and try to envision how he plummeted down the mountainside to achieve his current, unenviable position. Our calling out to him proves perfunctory, a waste of time in the howling gale. Don, if it is Don, doesn't give any indication he has seen us as we watch his headlamp bob about far below. Ron starts to walk down to him, leaving me to look after our two teams, when we get the impression he has spotted us. Then, Ron again with his team, we head out, assuming "Don" spots that as well. Once descended and approaching the bay, we stop and wait, but not for long. It *was* Don, he *did* spot us, and he has bushwhacked his way to the trail, and to us. Not eager to embarrass him by asking how he made such a navigational error, we don't ask, and he doesn't tell.

Sunset on the Sea Ice, Just out of Elim. Spruce Boughs Serve as Markers.

Finally on Golovin Bay, it's only a few flat, straight-arrow miles on the sea ice to Golovin itself. At some time in the race's future, Golovin will cease to be a real checkpoint and just a pass-through, where one can pause briefly to warm up and sip some coffee. Two or three times I will do that, and *need* to do that. Mt. McKinley involves vigorous exercise, again resulting in sweat-soaked clothes. When approaching Golovin on the ice, always in the dark and well below zero it seems, I get chilled to the bone. Knowing that beyond Golovin lurks two more hypothermic hours to White Mountain, the urge if not the necessity to take that pause becomes irresistible.

With Ron, Don and the others, the pause, though not compulsory, is much longer and more structured since in '79 Golovin *is* a checkpoint with the usual "drop bags" containing our dog food and other supplies—also a checker, a vet, pilots and other volunteers. In this case one pilot is Martin Olson, well known in these parts. Martin and his wife Maggie are the owners of the checkpoint building, which, besides their home, is also a store. We're dead to the world in that store for most of the night, until rudely aroused the next morning by the disagreeably loud, raspy voice of a talking Mynah bird, perched in its cage near my dead body on the roadhouse floor. When back to life and well into my second cup of coffee, I browse around and unearth all manner of relics from the old days, circa 1910. One is a small wooden sign with the inscription, HOT BATHS—FIRST WATER 15 CENTS, USED WATER 5 CENTS.

Photo Courtesy of the Harvey Fiskeaux Family, Nome

In the bright sunlight of a splendiferous new day, we prepare to depart Golovin. My dogs are all set to go, with one exception. One of my males has developed a sore foot, and he tells me he is no longer having much fun. I hate to leave him, but after more than 1000 miles he's only the second team member I've had to drop, so I say "See you later" and turn to my remaining eleven. That's plenty to get me to Nome, now less than 100 miles away. As I head for my sled I am greeted by something out of the ordinary. It's not my sled. I mean, I can't *see* my sled. It's obliterated by children, a whole bunch of 'em, sitting on it. Each urchin is smiling broadly and is more colorfully clad than the next. My team pulls them a short way, and then they get off and run ahead, leading me out of the village like a group of pied pipers.

Urchins

Led past Golovin's "main street" and pulled past the pipers, I'm back on the sea ice for another two hours of flat, trouble-free but wearisome sledding, until arriving at White Mountain. Confronting the boredom, I again sing to the dogs, review their names, or do most anything to avoid dozing off. Meanwhile, for the first few miles each dog engages in a routine, the daily dump. This involves every member of the team, but most telling are those at the rear, in front of the sled. When moving fast with feet flying, the musher gets pelted by poopy projectiles aplenty. Add the accompanying aroma, and you have an atmosphere akin to the changing of a diaper, something only a musher could love. A bright side to all this will be pointed out by Nic Petit, who rhymes, "Sixteen poopers, but no scoopers." In other words, you run the Iditarod with sixteen dogs pooping and no need for scooping, in contradistinction to life back in the kennel. That chore, besides being tedious, can even be dangerous as I will learn, again the hard way. Scooping will warrant the dubious distinction of leading to perhaps the most painful of all my sled dog injuries. On one particularly inauspicious kennel cleaning session, while shoveling I slip on the ice, land on the rim of a plastic poop bucket, and break two ribs.

The Pied Pipers of Golovin

Chapter Forty-Seven
SNAGS

By noon we're at White Mountain, after the monotonous Golovin Bay and then a short section on the Fish River. The village is situated high on the bank of that river, before it enters the sea. It was popularized by Johny Horton in his song *North to Alaska* as "White Mountain, just a little southeast of Nome…." There I spend some time in the home of Howard Lincoln, the face of the race in his community. I take a photo of Howard's granddaughter beside the family's woodstove. Boiling water has filled the room with steam so the young girl seems to be shrouded in fog. (Perhaps I will locate that pic too, someday.)

Outside, I'm on my knees, chopping up meat with an ax, when I hear, "Hi, Dad." It's my daughter, Margaret. She has flown from Nome to White Mountain in a plane piloted by Ray Lang, a dentist, musher, family friend and our host in Nome. I look up, get up, give Margaret a hug and snap the snapshot. It is heartwarming because I have not seen her since leaving Anchorage, more than three weeks ago.

Race rules specify that you have certain items in your sled—snowshoes, ax, cooker, adequate dog food, backup booties, sleeping bag, promotional material. They also specify that you take that twenty-four-hour break at a checkpoint of your choosing, chosen generally by midrace or sooner. A future rule will be an eight-hour stop at any checkpoint on the Yukon River, and then eight hours at White Mountain. These are good rules, benefiting the dogs by ensuring adequate rest at key points, and they have altered race tactics, especially the final eight. Zack Steer will say that the Iditarod is "A race to White Mountain," and there's some truth to that. Whichever team arrives there first almost always goes on to win, after its eight hours.

White Mountain

Margaret

After *our* eight hours (not the obligatory, just our routine) Ron, Don, Harry, Gene and I leave White Mountain in late afternoon, together. Inexplicably but somehow typically, we stop after less than ten miles. One of us understates that we're not really racing and should avail ourselves of a sentimental last time together round a campfire. The sun sets, a backdrop for some mountains, and we do share that time together as night comes on.

Mushing Toward the Campfire

If we were really racing we would have left White Mountain and run almost nonstop to Nome, ten hours on average, without significant snags. At best there are small snags, if you consider the many big Topkok hills as small, not to mention the blow holes, always a potential problem. Underlying everything is an intense weariness with a desire to get it over with, and the longing for a shower and a bed, and a beer. A few teams will "snag-out" on this last run and find themselves out of the race when they meet the ultimate mutiny, mostly in the days before enactment of the White Mountain rest rule. After our little campfire we enter those hills, the scene of several of the snagouts.

One snag, some details of which remain unclear to me, will nearly be my undoing. Early in that year's race, around Nikolai, I develop a troublesome blister on my left heel. Not to worry, I apply the cure-all duct tape and continue on my way, dismissing the blister from conscious thought. I don't "redress" it even once, but days later it begins to bark, as it were. By Koyuk I am limping and by White Mountain am limping badly, as well as feeling subpar in general. I can't sleep, although I desperately need to do so. Writing it off to something I ate, I rise from the sleepless floor and limp towards Nome. By the end of the Topkoks I've become disoriented, and I stop at the sight of a very familiar cabin, again one I've never seen before (?!). I presume, with cloudy conviction but incorrectly, that I have taken a wrong turn, even when another musher (Jessie Royer, I think) goes by me and dissolves into the night ahead. So I reverse direction and backtrack about an hour, revisiting those hills until I run head-on into another dog team. The rest is lost to me, as I can evoke only fragments of this forgettable episode, just enough to piece some of it together later. Upon reaching Nome and shedding boots, socks and the tape, I regard my heel as a swollen, pussy, bloody mess, and my leg with red streaks coursing up to the enlarged, tender lymph nodes in my groin. Dr. Paul Steer, Zack's father (vide supra, *Sports Illustrated*) renders a diagnosis of ascending lymphangitis, or in lay terms, blood poisoning. Why did *I* not figure that out? It could be because a doctor is his own worst patient, or because I was way too focused on my team to take a good look at myself, or even a poor look. I dunno. Anyway, the infection with its fever explains my malaise at White Mountain and my disorientation at Topkok. The admonition, "Physician, heal thyself," does not apply in my case, but the antibiotic given me by Dr. Steer does the trick. By the next day I'm a new man, and by the next hour I'm downing that beer at the Polar Bar.

Chapter Forty-Eight
WE RACE

The Camping Party, not really racing, is soon really racing, racing each other to trail's end. It's unspoken, but some spark of competition has arisen, as from the ashes of the campfire. Talk gets around to how long it will take to (race to) Nome and how few competitive minutes' headstart we should spot Gene, and us other four. Intraparty relationships have changed, no longer the gallant one for all and all for one.

Escaping those Topkok Hills, we level out on the shore of the Bering Sea, flat running for twenty miles to Safety, the last checkpoint prior to Nome. We come to Solomon, formerly a small community and also a checkpoint itself. It is the region of the Solomon Blow Hole. The ambient temperature is below zero, and a blow from the Hole makes me wish I were somewhere else. Exploring what remains of Solomon and keen for an opportunity to warm up, I head for an old building, mayhap a former store or restaurant, with Ron. Outside surroundings are stark, without as much as a bush anywhere. Within the building it is the same, without a single piece of wood for a fire in the old stove. Frost is overall and frames the structure as in the movie *Doctor Zhivago*. It feels even colder inside than out. In vain we try to fool ourselves that we're warmer, and then we're back on our sleds.

Topkok to Safety is one of the windswept, barren expanses where the trail can offer as much gravel, or sand or dirt, as snow. The sled moves along slowly but otherwise satisfactorily, and the dogs don't mind, having trod on lots of rough surfaces during their fall training; but the musher minds because the abrasive gravel does a number on the plastic attached to the underside of the sled runners.

Soon the plastic is severely scored, no longer gliding smoothly and slowing the going. In a future era that plastic will become rapidly removable, permitting its replacement quickly — in as little as ten minutes – providing you have a spare set in your sled. The same year as my infected foot and after my delirium tremendous at Topkok, my plastic (black, the weakest variety) will become not just scored but rent asunder. It comes off, off both of the runners. Without a spare (added evidence of a deranged mind) I press on, the sled grinding away on bare aluminum. I will later come to learn that another guy, Hugh Neff, became plasticless at about the same place. Hugh and I both grind the forty-some miles to Nome, and we discover that running on unshod aluminum alone is not all that bad.

Safety. Now only twenty-two miles to go, but first a final break. The Safety checkpoint is, in 1979, a still-standing, still-functioning roadhouse, one of the very few. I assume it was named for providing safe haven to old-time mushers who made it through the blow holes and other vicissitudes. I will feel privileged to have devoted some time here, since in a few years the old roadhouse will burn to the ground. For now, in the old edifice, I devote myself to some breakfast and coffee. Then to my team, and I'm on the trail for one final run.

Safety

Subsequent to the fiery destruction of the Safety roadhouse, a new "house" will take its place, complete with room, board and booze, but I will learn not to stop there, having nothing to do with the booze. If your tired dog team gets a whiff of the straw on which a few dropped dogs are lying in repose, it decides to be dropped too, and the decision can prove nearly irreversible. This manifests in about my third or fourth Iditarod when it becomes my distinct displeasure to walk my whole outfit about a mile, a long and frustrating mile, before the dogs move on their own volition, the aroma of the straw finally out of their little noses and noggins.

Resting and getting a good snootful at Safety—Cape Nome in the Background

Safety to Nome, "on the beach" or near enough to it in the early years of the race, is mostly flat, easy going. With the passage of time the beach will become the road not taken, the trail most commonly coursing "over the Cape." It takes a jog away from the seacoast and up the several hundred foot Cape Nome. For the musher, it's one last hurdle before the end, and the hurdle can be high, like the Topkok Hills. Twice I will have considerable trouble convincing my dogs that all they need do is pull my sorry, sore ass up that one last hill, necessitating my pulling with them or in front of them as lead dog once more. Summiting the Cape is worth the effort for its own sake. For one thing, it affords a comforting view at night when for the first time you feast on the welcoming lights of Nome, at a mere ten easy miles. For another, it affords your dogs the same view that, with the downhill and inherent easy sledding, perks them up and hastens to Front Street. Along the way are signs of civilization—roads, snowmachines, all terrain vehicles, cars, trucks and people, cheering and encouraging, further energizing your dog team.

In 2010, two things of note will occur. I am cruising along with about five miles to go, having passed one team hours earlier and with an apparent lock on twenty-third place, when I hear the prancing and pawing and panting of two dogs, then two more and then two more. It's Cim Smyth, his six-dog team passing my eleven like I'm standing still. I exhort my snails to speed up and stay with him, but without success. This comes as no surprise since Cim, like his brother Ramey, has the reputation of being unbeatable in the home-stretch, earned by routinely posting the fastest run from Safety to Nome. That's one thing. The other occurs only minutes later. As mentioned, I have passed several people, Nomites and tourists, race fans all. When nearing three more, at trailside and most anonymous, I am concentrating on Smyth, now some two hundred yards in front of me, and not on those three people. As I pass by them I utter perfunctorily, "How ya doin'?" which I follow up with a double take and, "Oh my God, it's you guys!" The three people turn out to be my wife Anna, son Jimmy and our Spanish exchange student, Guillermo. After a ten-day absence, all I had for them was that "How ya doin'?"

Chapter Forty-Nine
TRAIL'S END

Back to 1979 and the race unspoken but real. Just after leaving Safety I look around. No, not around. I look backwards and forwards. Backwards I see Ron and Gene Leonard, Ron at about 300 yards, Gene about five miles so I don't see him at all. (And as for backwards, I should mention another sight. At night, if a team is right on your tail, not hundreds of yards back, it appears as a stringy constellation of dancing stars, the dogs' eyes reflecting your headlamp. Very striking it is, if you've never beheld it before.) I've lost track of Don Montgomery, but forwards I catch sight of Hairy Harry. It's daytime, and the distant, dark silhouette of a dog team and its driver, something like a peace pipe, is unmistakable against its white background. Harry thus signals his location, and I give chase. Over the next few miles the pipe grows, and then I catch him, all in the spirit of friendly rivalry, or so I think. Harry Harris, however, a Nomite with friends and sponsors at home, wants those folks to see him finish first among the last. When Jim Lanier claims that meaningless honor, Harry will be pissed but won't show it until the next day. Then he comes up and accuses me of disgracing him thoughtlessly, and vows he will never speak to me again. True to his word, he doesn't, not for a quarter of a century, because we don't run into each other for a quarter of a century. Then, when I'm in Nome for another race, Harry not only speaks, he greets me warmly. Time heals.

As for the others, Don Montgomery fades from my radar into the TLC of his wife, as was the case in checkpoints during the race. I will see him in transit the next few days, and then Don will resume his executing in Ohio, his Iditarod mushing aspirations brought to fruition. I will never meet him again. Perhaps exclusive of other Iditarod veterans, Don's name will grace the trail, officially and everlastingly in the form of Don's Cabin, the cabin *Beyond Ophir* that he funded.

*My Kids—Margaret, Kim and Willy—Standing
O'er the Beach in Nome and Framing their Dad's
Approaching Peace Pipe*

Gene Leonard, an Iditarod legend if ever there should be one. It's not just his boxing background, his bar in the Bronx, his mushing, his booze hounds or his life in the bush with his mail-order bride. It's his character, exuding the energy, enthusiasm and élan that defined the man. He makes his grand entrance into Nome, as tall as a taildragger can be—not only king of our little party, but exemplary icon for the entire race, in my opinion (and perhaps in the opinion of Jon Van Zyle, the noted Iditarod artist, whose 1982 Iditarod poster is an iconic likeness of Gene Leonard). For his effort Gene receives the Red Lantern award, a genuine kerosene lantern, color red, which I expect he will display proudly in his quarters at Finger Lake. The idea of the Red Lantern, steeped in dog mushing lore, is that when finishing a race last and late, a lantern must be utilized to find one's way home in the dark. Surprising but true, last in the Iditarod can be a relatively prized position. As for the 1979 Lantern recipient, Gene Leonard will live many more years at Finger Lake, mushing the Iditarod three more times and other years serving as checkpoint host and checker, before retiring to Tennessee where he will meet his maker.

I'm the forty-third musher to enter Nome, triumphantly if not grandly, and even tentatively if you will, still not certain of Montgomery's standing. It has taken me twenty-four days and change, right up there amongst the longer travel times in Iditarod history, although the record is more than a week longer at thirty-two, by John Schultz in 1973. Twenty-four days is sufficiently long to feel almost alien to my family, gathered to greet me under the burled arch. Coming in off the Bering Sea and up onto Front Street, I can see the Nome National Forest (with the locals' Christmas trees jammed into the ice), also the site of Nome's goofy golf tournament (with colored golf balls, unnaturally). Once onto the street, it's a few city blocks to the arch with raucous crowds, cars, bars and other curbside enterprises. The running surface is often graveled pavement, regularly so if at the back of the pack, but at this point, *macht nichts*. The end is in sight, and I'm glad it's over. I suppose my family is glad, both to see me and that it's over. They span three generations, from the youngest, son Willy at age one, to my Dad, Wild Bill Lanier at age sixty-five. He shocks me completely, having flown unannounced from North Dakota. Under the arch, it is a great moment in sports with hugs and kisses all around—for me, for my family and friends, and for my dogs. An official checks my sled for the presence of my mandatory gear, and I linger for a brief interview with a guy from KNOM. Then I mush my dogs to the nearby Iditarod dog lot where I tether them, feed them and say goodnight.

A siren sounds, announcing the eminent arrival of another team. It's Ron, and his team is seen on Front Street. At first they are progressing, but then disaster strikes. Much as in the lead dog contest on Anchorage's Fourth

Avenue, Ron's lead dog spies a fire hydrant, or Nome equivalent, and goes for it. In a flash the entire team is off the street, up on the sidewalk, and wrapped around the equivalent. Everybody, including the drunks, urge Ron to get his team straightened out, and he eventually does so but for a few minutes provides high comedy for all. In another few minutes he mushes under the burled arch to be congratulated by race officials, his family and me, and Ron and I light up a victory cigar.

Finish Line with the Burled Arch on Front Street in Nome

My Welcoming Committee

Almost the End

The End

Disaster

Victory

Hairy

Well, that's about it. As indicated, I will not maintain contact with Don, Harry or Gene. Not intentionally, it will just happen that way. Ron and I, conversely, will remain mutually supportive friends and mushing mates for the rest of Ron's life, which will end too soon but not for another twenty-five years. Ron will run the Iditarod one more time, in 1983 with his son Rob.

After the finish, the cigar and the bedding down of my dogs, I am ready for a bedding myself, but not before a beer at one of Nome's celebrated saloons. Thirst things first, I always say. And then, ensconced in my hosts' home, I do find a bed and make use of it. Sleep, though immediate and deep, is not long, on the order of only four or five hours. After twenty-four days on the trail, you would think I could do better; and I do so but in installments, with lots of peculiar dreams and schemes. In between, in my nearly as peculiar wakeful state, I'm not normal either, not for several days. I maintain that as many days are required to recover fully as the number of days raced, and I never return to work or make weighty decisions (such as whether I will enter the Iditarod next year) for a minimum of ten days after the end of the race, preferably while some tropical paradise like Hawaii mends my wounds—physical, mental and spiritual. But Nome is ideal for kicking off the healing process. It's small, only about 9,000 souls, and the defining part of it, along the seacoast, can be covered quickly on foot. Most everybody knows everybody, and a stranger doesn't remain one very long. I will make many friends there, e.g. my hosts over the years: Ray and Carla Lang, Doug and Lori Lange, Dottie Pinkney, Lieudell and Carmile Goldberry, and Harvey and Nancy Fiskeaux.

Gene

In 1979 the healing inaugurates my tradition of Nome "vacations," the few days expended there before boarding an Alaska Airlines jet bound for Anchorage. I walk around town, not like a tourist but as a *Finisher, a* musher who has *finished* all 1049 miles. This first time has taken me those twenty-four days, ten more than Rick Swenson's victory in fourteen. (In years ahead, the race will be won in only nine days, and even less.) So I have missed out on most of the end-of-race celebrations and festivities: the "Meet the Musher" autograph session, the Finishers' Club meeting, pancake feeds, crab feeds, reindeer feeds, golf and basketball tourneys and, most of all, hanging out at race headquarters, not to mention the bars. My children will have an equally awesome time in Nome, and Jimmy will come to feel he has partly grown up there. In '79 many of our traditions have not even begun, one of them being singing at the Church of the Proximity (that Covenant church immediately adjacent the arch) and another, our songs at the end of race banquet. At the end of my first Iditarod, I'm so tardy that I miss the banquet altogether, the first banquet that is. Never short on hospitality, the Nome Iditarod folks host a second banquet, or a third if necessary, which is the case for the Executive Camping Party. There we tell our "tales of the trail" and receive a few congratulatory awards and certificates, like Gene Leonard's Red Lantern. Most coveted is the Iditarod Finisher's belt buckle, proudly and regularly displayed on the waist of many a race veteran. I am no exception, my pants often held up by my buckled belt. Come 1984, my second Iditarod, I will "swim" to Nome in seventeen days, cutting a whole week off my 1979 time. As exhausted as ever, I put up with the swimming, some frostbite and the discouragement of again coming in no better than fortieth. By the banquet, a second banquet this time, I'm looking forward to receiving, if nothing else, a second buckle. I cannot overemphasize my disappointment and dismay when I'm told that each musher is awarded a buckle only once, at the completion of his or her *first* race. I must, however, make a final confession here. I *do* receive a second belt buckle, by oversight in 1999, and I've still got it. Iditarod officials may want it returned, but they will need to wrench it from my cold, dead hands.

EPILOG(UE)

The belt buckle is not my only incentive for coming back, mushing to Nome, time after time. It's the same for many others who can't seem to get enough misery. Is it for the money? Partly, for those who earn a decent year-round living off the sport, also for the fourteen thousand dollars my Mushathon raised for the Providence Thermal Unit. (For me, it's more like in *spite* of the money, the money *spent*.) Is it for fame? Partly, for those who become famous. Is it for making it to Nome? Maybe. And for some people, it's not just for getting to *Nome*. In 1977 Bud Smyth (running the entire race disguised as the Russian Vasily Zamitkyn) detoured around the dog lot to the end of town, and then headed west for the Bering Straits, Russia and "home" (but for only a few hundred yards—end of charade). I played a different variation on that same tune in 1996 when I loaded my team on a Bering Air Cargo prop plane and took off with them for the Nadyezshda (Hope) Sled Dog Race in the Russian Far East. An exciting epic, but again, that's another story.

End of Trail, End of Day in Nome, and End of Book.